Raising Resilient Children with a Borderline or Narcissistic Parent

Raising Resilient Children with a Borderline or Narcissistic Parent

Margalis Fjelstad and Jean McBride

ROWMAN & LITTLEFIELD
Lanham • Boulder • New York • London

Published by Rowman & Littlefield
An imprint of The Rowman & Littlefield Publishing Group, Inc.
4501 Forbes Boulevard, Suite 200, Lanham, Maryland 20706
www.rowman.com

6 Tinworth Street, London SE11 5AL, United Kingdom

British Library Cataloguing in Publication Information Available

Library of Congress Cataloging-in-Publication Data

Names: Fjelstad, Margalis, 1945- author. | McBride, Jean, 1947- author.
Title: Raising resilient children with a borderline or narcissistic parent / Margalis Fjelstad and Jean McBride.
Description: Lanham : Rowman & Littlefield, [2020] | Includes bibliographical references and index. | Summary: "Children can be negatively affected emotionally by a narcissistic or borderline parent, but the other parent can do a lot to mitigate those effects by using compassion, open communication, honesty, validation, and unique problem-solving skills. The authors provide research-based insight and   information that is invaluable to parents to increase their inner strength and self-confidence, so they can protect their children from adverse consequences and teach them to develop emotional insulation,   courage, self-confidence, and resilience"—Provided by publisher.
Identifiers: LCCN 2019048505 (print) | LCCN 2019048506 (ebook) | ISBN 9781538127636 (paper : alk. paper) | ISBN 9781538127643 (epub) Subjects: LCSH: Narcissism. | Parent and child. | Resilience (Personality trait) in children. | Parenting.
Classification: LCC BF575.N35 F5399 2020 (print) | LCC BF575.N35 (ebook) | DDC 649/.63—dc23
LC record available at https://lccn.loc.gov/2019048505
LC ebook record available at https://lccn.loc.gov/2019048506

Every child who winds up doing well has had at least one stable and committed relationship with a supportive adult.

—National Scientific Council on the Developing Child

Contents

Part III: Parenting Will Be Different

Author's Note

All of the examples, anecdotes, and characters in this book are drawn from our clinical work, research, and life experiences with real people and events. Names and some identifying events and details have been changed, and some situations are composites to protect people's privacy.

~

Introduction

As a parent you naturally have a strong desire to raise your children to be happy, healthy, self-confident, and resilient. However, you have now found yourself in a family environment with a self-absorbed partner who is frequently negative, chaotic, hostile, confusing, and overwhelming. He or she seems to constantly be in a different reality—easily upset about normal, everyday events, making irrational demands, constantly dissatisfied with you and the children, and always changing the rules. One minute everything seems normal and rational, the next minute everything explodes—seemingly for no discernable reason.

You repeatedly find yourself at odds with each other. Your partner seems to have changed since you first got together. Your relationship used to feel happy, intense, and so full of promise, while now you hardly know the person you're presently parenting with. It's so different that sometimes you feel scared that you're losing your mind. You don't know if your relationship will last, even though you're working hard to keep everything together.

Family life is different when you have a partner with narcissistic or borderline characteristics. Typical parenting and relationship strategies don't fit your situation. You think you're on the same page with the other parent, but suddenly she or he goes completely off script, saying and doing things that are out of line with what you expected or agreed to. Conflicts seem to come out of nowhere and too often never get resolved. They're overly dramatic, and throw the whole family into turmoil. You've heard from the experts that parents need to work together, be consistent, and present a "united front," but you're finding that is nearly impossible to do. The other parent often seems so emotionally unhinged, you're constantly confused about whether to stand with your partner or step in to protect the children against him or her.

This book offers a different kind of parenting strategy for your very different kind of situation. As therapists, we've worked for years with families like yours. People with narcissistic and borderline traits perceive and respond to the world and life's stresses in quite different and often unproductive ways. They're overly intense, see everything only from their own perspective, misinterpret many social cues, and respond stridently. Their expectations for your children are often self-centered, inconsistent, and unrelated to the child's needs or abilities. As a result, it's hard to figure out what's going on or how to change things so your family can get back to the "normal" that you expected.

We understand the difficulties of parenting with a person who is deeply self-absorbed in their own skewed reality. We have each worked for over thirty years with families like yours. To parent effectively with a person who has narcissistic or borderline behaviors is NOT intuitive. It often requires you to act very differently than you would expect to interact in a normal relationship. You can't always follow the typical advice of marriage counselors or parenting experts.

This book is designed to help you understand what you can do to help your children thrive, despite your less-than-favorable family patterns. Our focus is to show you how to develop resilience, courage, self-esteem, and self-compassion in yourself and your children so you can help them succeed and blossom into the unique and special people they're meant to be. We want to help you keep your eye on the healthy development and needs of your children rather than getting enmeshed and side-tracked into caretaking the other parent at your children's expense. This book provides an emotional prescription that shows you how to teach your children to cope with this very difficult family situation and still develop into healthy, competent, and joyful people, and at the same time keep yourself grounded and emotionally healthy.

Your challenge as a parent with an emotionally unstable partner is to handle yourself with strength and compassion without becoming angry and overbearing and also avoid passivity and weak-heartedness. It's a tricky balance that takes courage, accurate perceptions, and unique skills. You'll need to keep your body and mind healthy and sharp, and to do that you'll need *lots* of support. Your goal is to raise your children to be healthy, resilient individuals, while at the same time tempering the oftentimes unbalanced responses from the narcissistic or borderline parent.

Growing up with a parent who has borderline or narcissistic personality disorder can be a challenging experience, but it doesn't have to be a guaranteed disaster. Your children's experiences can be greatly enhanced by your attitude and how you handle the situation. You can do a great deal to help your children understand what's going on, mitigate disastrous interactions with the emotionally unstable parent, and enhance their overall development. Our goal is to give you the information you need to parent effectively in your unique and challenging family system so you can provide a calmer, more secure, and happier childhood for your children, and they can develop into compassionate, competent, caring, and courageous individuals.

Margalis Fjelstad, PhD, LMFT
Jean McBride, MS, LMFT

PART I

WHEN THE OTHER PARENT IS NARCISSISTIC OR BORDERLINE

CHAPTER ONE

~

Self-Focused Parenting

The kind of parenting and family patterns that you're experiencing and trying to cope with aren't ideal for helping your children grow to their fullest potential. Working with a narcissistic parent (NP) or a borderline parent (BP) means that you are also coping with their deficiencies in rational thinking, emotional overreactivity, self-focused thinking, anxiety, depression, and confusion—in addition to trying to attend to the needs of your children. These problems impact how your family functions, including the expectations and rules you establish and how you and the narcissistic or borderline parent interact. It is very difficult to see what's happening in your family when you're in the middle of it.

Personality Disorders

Personality disorders are the most pervasive mental illnesses throughout the world. In the United States alone approximately 15 percent to 19 percent of the population or between forty-nine million and sixty-two million people show evidence of a personality disorder.[1] Narcissistic Personality Disorder (NPD) and Borderline Personality Disorder (BPD) are the most prevalent. Personality disordered *traits* and *behaviors* appear in an even larger proportion of the population.

NPD and BPD don't have symptoms that can be fixed with medication or even ordinary talk therapy. They consist of patterns of traits and behaviors that are the result of dysfunctions in the brain as well as poor parenting, years of being rewarded and given in to for their selfish demands and tantrums, and sometimes traumatic childhood events. People with narcissistic and borderline behaviors have a range of mild to severe problems, including how they perceive, emotionally respond, and understand personal interactions. Their ability to adapt to new situations, be flexible when situations change, or learn from their mistakes is severely impaired. Their adaptive tool set is limited to a very few rigid responses. They persist in the same responses over and over, even when they meet failure or receive negative feedback. In interpersonal relationships, they can't see cause and effect, nor can they effectively problem solve. NP/BPs give up, blame you or others for their failures, and demand that you change or fix the problem for them.

Causes

How does this dysfunction happen? For years it was believed that these problems were completely the result of trauma and/or poor parenting. Recent research at the Karolinska Institute in Sweden using their twin registry of over eighty-five thousand twins concludes that personality is 75 percent inherited.[2] Borderline personality is 78 percent to 95 percent inherited, and narcissism is 77 percent inherited. You inherited most of your personality as well. You may have noticed that other members of your NP/BP partner's family have many of the same traits and behaviors. It's well known that BPD and NPD runs in families.

Of course, lifetime experiences offer opportunities that can either help or hinder innate personality patterns. People with healthy personalities become more and more flexible and adaptable over time because they can see what does and doesn't work and they make changes to be more successful. However, the dysfunctions in brain functioning of the NP/BP act as a hinderance to his/her ability to learn new patterns and adapt to new circumstances. NP/BPs interpret even small setbacks and difficulties as overwhelming difficulties, so they give up and find excuses for why they shouldn't have to change or alter their behavior.

Observing Ego Is Missing or Impaired

Essentially the NP/BP doesn't have a well-functioning Observing Ego. That's the part of your mind that tells you when you're making a mistake, assesses new situations, sees and understands other people's reactions, and makes suggestions to help you change and make better choices. This is missing, damaged, or very minimal in the NP/BP.

With a limited Observing Ego, NP/BPs lack the ability to observe their own behaviors, understand other people's feelings, or see how their behaviors affect others. So, even when you tell them how they are hurting you or the children, the NP/BP doesn't know what you're talking about. It's as if they're emotionally blind and deaf because they can't see the connection between their behaviors and other's feelings and reactions. They literally don't believe they have done anything wrong or inappropriate. Instead, they assume you're wrong or crazy.

Persistent Patterns

As a result, the NP/BP learns very slowly and primarily through behavior modification rather than explanation or words. They have highly persistent patterns of behavior, so you need to keep in mind that even though the NP/BP may say they understand or they will change, inevitably they'll revert to their previous responses. Talking doesn't help them change. You have to change what you do, so you give them different options and choices.

Predictable

Because their abilities and responses are so limited, you can learn to predict how they'll react. They often seem unpredictable because you didn't know or you forgot that they won't react like you or other normal people would. Perhaps you've even said, "I would never do that to someone. I would never say something like that. What's the matter with you?" You know something is wrong, but it's hard to understand or even believe.

Self-Focus

The NP/BP focuses primarily on their own thoughts, beliefs, feelings, and needs. They can't understand you or read many social cues because they can't see things from anyone else's perspective. Therefore, the NP/

BP will continually respond in odd, but predictably rigid, ways. Because you're more flexible and adaptable, you'll have a tendency to try to work around them and adjust to their needs and deficits. If you're not conscious and attentive, your family will become governed and limited by the NP/BP's inadequacies.

However, when you know the patterns and can see their effects on your children, there is a lot you can do to stabilize and neutralize the consequences of the NP/BP's behavior. Here are the common family patterns that develop when a parent has narcissistic or borderline traits.

Overt Narcissistic Parenting[3]

Few people are formally diagnosed with Narcissistic Personality Disorder or Borderline Personality Disorder, but many people exhibit strong borderline or narcissistic behaviors and traits. These include:

- extreme emotional reactions
- self-involved thinking
- high need for attention
- lack of empathy
- controlling and devaluing of others
- emotional inaccessibility
- difficulty caring for others
- impossible demands on their loved ones

Whether they have the real ability to love others is continually debated, however, they do have a strong need to be in attached relationships and deeply fear abandonment. This causes a pattern of wanting and seeking to be together all the time, along with a corresponding anxiety about being suffocated, so they push you away with anger and criticism. Of course, this pull/push pattern causes a great deal of emotional pain and instability in your family.

NP/BP Expectations

The NP/BP expects all their needs, feelings, and wants to be fulfilled by you and the children. Some of the time your partner can focus on the children—especially for play or entertainments that the NP/BP enjoys.

They may also be overly involved in the children's performance and the family's reputation in the community. However, most of the time attending to the children, taking them places, and accommodating their emotions and developing psyches are treated as drudgery and are accompanied by numerous complaints. For example, one client said that her narcissistic husband expected to be paid to "babysit" their children whenever she was out of the house.

Can't Tune into Others
Parents with borderline or narcissistic traits spend so much of their time thinking about their own emotional hurts, angers, and resentments that they really don't have much energy or patience to consider the needs and feelings of anyone else, even their children.

The NP/BP typically shows a severe lack of empathy for others.[4] Their lack of empathy includes an inability to appropriately read facial cues, understand that others have different feelings, or even comprehend the logic of other people's thoughts and emotional reactions. They simply believe that their own thoughts and feelings are, and should be, exactly matched by others close to them. When presented with statements from you or the children that you really do think and feel differently, the NP/BP merely concludes that you're wrong, and he/she may even get angry. They just can't see individual differences.

Demands Your Full Attention
The NP/BP has an extreme need for attention and emotional energy directed toward themselves. They often feel resentful when your attention is directed toward your work, friends, family, and even toward the children. They may follow you around the house, interrupt you, or demand instant attention for an "emergency," like finding their keys, even when you're attending to something important.

Overcontrolling or Neglectful Parenting
Their parenting behaviors tend to be either demanding and controlling or extremely lassez-faire or neglectful. They may get overinvolved in directing everything one child says or does and completely ignore and be unaware of the other children. They alternate between overregulating and inattention, creating confusion for everyone. Their blaming,

criticism, and random expectations appear according to *their* moods, which leaves the children—and you—confused about how to respond or what is real or true about what they say or do.

This parenting pattern is called *overt narcissistic parenting*. It's highly self-involved, often hurtful, and unresponsive to the children's growth and development. It's the result of the emotional disabilities and limitations of a parent with pervasive borderline or narcissistic traits.

Overtly, self-involved parenting behaviors *also* occur in families when a parent has an alcohol or drug addiction, is physically or sexually abusive, is severely religiously condemning and demanding, has other types of severe mental disorders, or has a serious secret—for example, illegal behavior, or a hidden sexual identity.

Covert Narcissistic Parenting

The less-obvious kind of self-involved parenting is *covert narcissistic parenting*. This pattern often occurs when you're in a relationship with someone who has less intense or less pervasive narcissistic or borderline traits. However, their behaviors can still be disruptive, erratic, and overly self-involved. Even though you have concerns for your children's well-being, your deep entanglement in a very complicated relationship with someone with these significant emotional difficulties means that you probably feel a strong compulsion to caretake them as well. You may find yourself caretaking them to keep the peace, to maintain the relationship, to try to "fix" them, or to figure out how to extricate yourself and leave because you want to mitigate the negative effects of his or her behaviors on your children.

When you become the caretaker to an NP/BP, you'll find yourself spending a great deal of time and energy focused on his or her difficult behaviors rather than on your children. In hard terms, you are literally choosing between the needs of the other parent and those of your children. This leads to *covert narcissistic parenting*. Your need to placate and maintain the relationship takes precedence over your children's needs. This may seem shocking or horrifying to contemplate. However, when you're in a family with a such a selfish and manipulative partner, you may feel you have no choice. We want to help you see that you actually do have choices and how to use them as much as possible for the healthy development of your children.

Narcissistic Family System

The authors of *The Narcissistic Family* say that whenever the needs of the parents dominate the energy and focus of the whole family, they consider it a narcissistic family system or NFS.[5] The narcissistic family system doesn't have to have a diagnosed narcissist or borderline parent. It's a family in which the needs of the parents and their marital system consistently come before the needs of the children. This can be due to the mental health problems of one of the parents, continuing conflict between the parents, a disinterest in parenting by one or both parents, a high need for control and dominance over the children, extremely high personal goals of the parents, underlying hostility between the parents, and addiction.

The NFS can look good on the outside, and it may even seem well functioning on the inside, too. Adults go to work, children are physically healthy, well dressed and well fed, the parents participate in the community, and the home is well taken care of. However, what doesn't work in the NFS is the healthy, emotional development of the children. Without positive attention and extra help, children in these families have difficulty handling stress, adapting to change, setting realistic goals, problem solving, and maintaining intimacy because they don't observe or learn healthy responses from this family dynamic.

NFS Effects on Children

The Narcissistic Family System can leave children with problems such as:

- poor self-image, feelings of insignificance
- difficulty trusting themselves or others
- a sense of emptiness
- feelings of being unloveable
- people pleasing
- passivity
- buried anger

- lack of confidence, follow through, and/or motivation
- fear of intimacy, yet a desperate need for intimacy
- guilt, fear
- out of touch with their own feelings, thoughts, and wants
- overly self-demanding, perfectionistic
- lack assertion, difficulty protecting their boundaries and rights
- poor leadership and problem-solving skills

These symptoms may not show up until adulthood, when children who seemed so well behaved become workaholics, depressed, anxious, have continually failing relationships, or even covert addictions.[6] Other times, children from these families may show *early* signs of an inability to handle stress—including poor school performance, lack of friends, withdrawal, acting out, early drinking and sex, lack of trust in adults, and generally rebellious behavior.

Children from narcissistic family systems continually seem to stumble, make poor personal choices, and feel like failures throughout their lives even when things seem to be going well on the surface. They can lack the resilience needed to face the difficulties and challenges of adult life, they often give up too easily, and make poor life decisions.

As the caretaking parent, you've probably tried to cover up your difficulties and conflicts with the NP/BP, hoping these problems wouldn't affect the children. You are already working hard to keep your family together "for the sake of the children." You try to please and appease your self-involved, emotionally unstable partner. You give in to the NP/BP's demands to keep him/her from causing more conflict and chaos. It's all so confusing and often overwhelming. It's truly hard to see how the rules and expectations in your family could result in this kind of emotional damage to your children. After all, you would obviously choose to raise your children to be self-confident, independent, happy, resilient, and successful in life, rather than have them struggle emotionally and stumble through poor decisions.

It's really challenging to see the reality of what's going on in the narcissistic family system. Because the NP/BP is so very out of touch with reality and also demands that you agree with him/her on everything, you can get deeply confused and lost in their fantasy thinking and skewed logic without even noticing. Here are some clues to look for.

Narcissistic Family System Rules

The rules in the NFS can be hard to figure out. They're convoluted, often secret, don't seem to really make sense, and may frequently contradict each other. Instead of being designed to promote healthy development and positive interactions, NFS family rules are designed to protect the fragile ego and needs of the NP/BP. In other words, rules and patterns are intended to keep the family system functioning despite an emotionally disturbed and disabled parent.

In healthy, securely connected families, the rules are often very simple. The primary rule is *Don't do anything to hurt yourself or others*, which applies to the parents as well as the children. All other behaviors flow from that one rule. In the NFS, the primary rule is: *Do whatever you need to do in order to keep the NP/BP happy*. This results in dozens of expectations and mini rules for you and the children that can be difficult to follow. Here's an overview of some of the common rules and culture of the NFS:

- Rules only apply to the children. Adults can always break the rules.
- Children's needs and requests are randomly responded to, often ignored, or discounted, and frequently make the parents frustrated or angry.
- Real, personal feelings are not discussed and usually denied or discounted.
- Parents' needs come first; for example, children are ignored while the parents fight with each other, appease the angry partner, break routines, try not to "rock the boat," forget to pick up the children, cancel plans at the last minute, get hurt, depressed and withdraw, and never solve issues.
- Parents expect the children to act more maturely than they do.
- Communication is vague, indirect, and often involves secret codes; for example, saying yes when you mean no; saying forget it when you mean do it; expecting others to read your mind; pretending you're happy when you're really angry or depressed; talking more politely when you're really furious; advice giving when others want you to listen.

- Parents are frequently too busy or distracted to notice children's needs, interests, and problems.
- Children have no right to participate in making rules.
- Children have little or no right to privacy.
- Parents pretend everything about the family is perfect.
- Everyone has to give in and agree with the narcissist/borderline parent.
- Parents seek reassurance from their children rather than giving reassurance.

How many of these behaviors happen automatically in your family? Which ones haven't you really noticed before? Seeing how your family is functioning can be discouraging at first, but having a clear picture of what's going on will help you discover and choose new parenting responses that can be really helpful to your children's well-being. You can create a warmer and more attentive atmosphere for your children—but not by following these rules.

Caretaker Role

As the more adaptable and flexible parent, you're constantly pulled and pushed back and forth, having to choose each moment whether to caretake the NP/BP or care for the children. The NP/BP wants your attention 24/7 as their audience and fan club. They can be jealous and dismissive of any time and attention you give to the children—except to keep them quiet, behaving well, and not bothering them. Since the NP/BP's parenting is often erratic and contaminated with unrealistic expectations, demands, and ignorance about the needs of children, you feel responsible to constantly look out for the children as well.

In the NFS, your job as caretaker of the whole system is primarily to keep the system going. You have to be hypervigilant to the wants of the NP/BP to avoid a meltdown or rage attack, while you're simultaneously worrying about the children. Quite honestly, you can't be a full-time caretaker to everyone and everything.

Putting Yourself First

You and the other parent are both adults. The number-one job of every adult is to take care of themselves. However, you're taking care of everything in order to keep the whole family system going, so it's imperative that you stay healthy, strong, and of sound mind. Taking care of your mental, physical, and emotional well-being takes time, energy, and money. As a responsive and caring person, it's likely that you're putting yourself last. This needs to be turned around if you're going to be successful in this difficult family environment. You need to get plenty of sleep, eat healthy food, get exercise, and deal quickly with any feelings of anxiety or depression.

Choosing Your Children

Your number-two job is to take care of the children you've brought into the world. Since the NP/BP's parenting skills and/or motivation are limited, you have double the job of figuring out how to parent well *and* create a healthy psychological environment for your children's development. This whole book is about supporting you to do that. In addition, we believe that raising your children to feel secure, competent, loving, and resilient human beings is an amazingly healing experience for you as well.

What is *not* your job is trying to fix, teach, or cure the NP/BP's behaviors or feelings. In fact, you have *no power* to control or change them in any way. You can expend an immense amount of energy trying to make them different, but we've never seen anyone be successful. That's a job for them to do—if they choose. Every moment you use up trying to heal or fix the NP/BP is a moment taken away from your own and your children's health and well-being.

Can you see how focusing so much worry and effort on the NP/BP conflicts and interferes with your ability to parent your children well? Do you want to focus on keeping your relationship intact with an emotionally dysfunctional person while your children flounder in life, or do you want to invest your energy where it will make a lifelong difference—parenting your children well? We think that picking up this book and reading this far means you've already decided to do your best to help your children weather the challenges and difficulties of having a narcissistic/borderline parent, and to come out of that experience whole, healthy, confident, self-compassionate, and resilient.

CHAPTER TWO

~

What the Narcissistic Family Is Like for Children

Human beings are very resilient. We can survive incredibly difficult, even horrific childhood experiences, and go on to live normal, well-adjusted lives as adults. It's one of the most encouraging and hopeful findings about resilience. Abuse and trauma are risk factors, but they aren't the single *cause* of later emotional instability or mental illness. Regardless, all parents spend most of their time working to diminish risks, suffering, and pain for their children and increase positive opportunities.

Children who grow up in NFS families definitely face emotional challenges. They are at risk of not getting critical needs met at significant points in their development. As a parent, you will need to be more attentive to the needs of your children that are not being met by the NP/BP. You may need to step in to offer help, or find others to fill in such as grandparents, aunts, uncles, coaches, teachers, friends, and others. With support, you can do a great deal to provide the support, love, nurturance, and social learning that your children need, even with a debilitated partner-parent.

Family Environment

In families that don't revolve around a parent with NPD or BPD, children typically receive ongoing encouragement and loving attention from both parents who validate their individuality and accomplishments. They grow up with clear and fair boundaries, so they don't have to guess about what the rules are and what is expected of them. This creates an environment where children learn that their parents and the smaller world of their family are emotionally and physically safe zones. Much like making a regular deposit to a savings account, each time children experience validation and emotional safety from parents, their "trust account" grows. In healthy families, these important deposits happen thousands of times in day-to-day experiences. It could be as simple as a smile or hug when a child is upset, to a somewhat more complex conversation where a child's feelings are heard and validated.

Each time a parent behaves in a kind, positive, and predictable manner, a child's trust grows. And then when children venture away from their family into the larger worlds of daycare, school, extended family and friends, they carry inside themselves a solid core of trust and security, which prepares them to more effectively handle the challenges that come as part of stepping into the larger world. When challenges come along, children know they have loving, supportive, and trustworthy resources at home to help them deal with whatever has happened.

Luckily, children don't have to have two perfect parents to develop into healthy, well-adjusted, loving people, and besides, there really is no such thing as a perfect parent. You only have to be "good enough" to help your children navigate the challenges that come up, and support their natural drive to learn, absorb, and discover how they fit into the world. Even though the NP/BP has significant deficits, they will still have some positive abilities. In addition, you can learn to be prepared to neutralize as much of the negativity as possible, as well as pull in other supportive relatives and friends to add resources. Remember, your children learn and grow with the help of many, many people during their developmental years.

Difficulties within the NFS

When children have a parent who is only partially or haphazardly able to provide emotional support, they're going to need a lot more kindness, reassurance, information, and encouragement from you to fill in the void. Because of the NP/BP's difficulty responding to new and challenging situations, she/he often reacts with highly charged emotional outbursts and rigid demands. Therefore, in NFS families the children's basic emotional needs of safety, security, and trust are frequently not met adequately.

Therapists, researchers, and authors who work with narcissistic families have used a number of terms to describe what it feels like for individuals in the family. Author Randi Kreger calls it "walking on eggshells."[1] Others have used terms like "living in a black hole, living in a tornado, we have a crazy house, surreal, scary, or unreal." These are powerful words that describe the chaos children and adults often experience in NFS families.

Effects of a Borderline Parent on Their Children

Christine Lawson[2] has described many of the impacts on children who have a borderline parent. Children tend to internalize the low self-esteem of the borderline parent, which can lead to an overall feeling of hopelessness and depression. Children see the continual unhappiness of the parent, no matter what the child does to try to make them smile, and they begin to feel they can never make the parent happy. They feel inadequate and lacking, and they may even feel guilty for being happy around the borderline parent. They learn early they can't trust the parent's moods or reactions, so they're often in a state of stress and anxiety around the parent.

Roseanne

When Roseanne was coming home from school, she never knew if she'd find her mother lying in the dark in her bedroom, in a screaming fit about Roseanne not doing her chores well enough, or baking cookies and being affectionate. Roseanne often had a knot in her stomach and found it hard to eat dinner. She tried to forget the bad times and only remember and think about the good times, but then she was often startled when her mother's moods suddenly spiked into anger and hostility again. She felt she couldn't trust other people's feelings or promises.

Children often report feeling unloved by the borderline parent, and believe it's due to some deficit in themselves. The love they get from the parent is so random, they don't feel they can rely on it. Even when the parent is loving, it's too often extremely sentimental. Since these children don't get much reliable affection, they often have difficulty feeling love or even liking for the borderline parent, and they usually feel quite guilty for this.

Marnie

Marnie, a software designer, dreaded holidays, especially Mother's Day and Christmas, when her mother expected Marnie to bring a wonder-ful, gushy card and be especially affectionate and admiring. Marnie described her mother's hugs as "draining" and "wearisome." She felt her mother was actually extracting energy from her rather than provid-ing caring and love. She could see her mother's need to be cared for but felt exhausted and even secretly angry about it. Marnie had moved two thousand miles away so that her contacts with her mother were infrequent, but she always left these encounters hurt, disappointed, and completely spent.

Children are aware that the BP parent is often unable to function adequately and will often step in to take care of the parent or the task at hand, essentially taking on a parenting role. Older children may take on caring for younger children, cooking, cleaning, and even giving up school activities to be at home to care for the parent who is lonely and depressed. They learn not to expect help from the borderline parent, resulting in their denying or repression of their own needs. In adult relationships, they may find it difficult to ask for love and support and feel resentful when they don't get it, or they automatically assume the role of caretaker.

Children of a borderline parent often end up feeling:[3]

- suffocated, controlled, and trapped
- shame, guilt, anxiety, rage
- self-destructive
- fearful, confused, crazy
- unable to identify NORMAL
- no one to turn to for comfort or support
- lost and alone

As the healthier parent, you can do a lot to step in and mitigate these effects on your children. When you notice negative emotional impacts, you can give positive, supportive, and caring responses. You can also provide information about the other parent's disabilities and explain that your children didn't cause these malfunctions. Later chapters will give you more ideas about these kinds of interventions.

Effects of a Narcissistic Parent on Their Children

Narcissistic parents tend to have a more subtle, hidden effect on their children. They can have bouts of anger and blaming, but it's their covert expectations of perfection, obedience, and superiority that affect their children the most. Children of narcissistic parents typically feel "never good enough." They feel like they never measure up. They often feel hurt, humiliated, and angry due to the unrealistic demands and control of the NP parent. They may desperately try to please the NP parent, alternating with giving up or even open rebellion.

A narcissistic parent often chooses a "favorite" child who is expected to be a mini-me clone. The narcissist puts a lot of extra pressure on this child to perform and meet the NP's hopes and dreams. This child may also get a lot of special treatment; for example, being given adult privileges without responsibilities, special presents, bending of the rules, but also being controlled, overprotected, and expected to merge their identity with the parent.

Adam

After having three daughters, Adam's narcissistic father expected him to be his "little man." His dad gave him everything he wanted, but in exchange he monopolized Adam's every thought and action. Adam wasn't allowed to ride a bike because he might fall and break his leg like his father had as a child. Yet he was given an expensive new car for his sixteenth birthday. Adam learned early how to please his dad, but at the same time he also learned how to sneak around and lie so he could do things he wanted with his friends.

Although Adam felt lucky to get so much attention and so many special gifts that his sisters didn't get, he often felt angry and disappointed. He really felt alone. He knew he was supposed to become a lawyer like his dad, but he just didn't have a sense of enthusiasm for college. He didn't have any really close friends partly because he didn't trust people, and he didn't feel very comfortable around women, whom he saw as inferior and boring. And he couldn't figure out why he didn't really like his dad or actually enjoy being around him. Everything just seemed so tedious and confusing.

On the other hand, children who aren't the favorite of a narcissistic parent may end up with little or no relationship with that parent who is too busy with his/her own interests and activities to pay much attention. These children primarily experience criticism, demands, and negligence. As a result, they may long for attention, but also fear it. And often, one child is singled out by the NP as a scapegoat for his/her anger, contempt, and blame. Demands on this child are often unrealistic, and no amount of compliance seems to be enough.

The common results of having a narcissistic parent include:[4]

- dysfunctional emotional understanding
- struggle with appropriate boundaries
- fail to recognize healthy romantic partners
- fall into a caretaker role and people pleasing
- difficulty trusting their feelings and thoughts
- struggle with self-esteem
- prone to addictions
- may develop narcissistic behaviors themselves

Trying to mitigate a narcissistic parent's on-again/off-again, push/pull, adoration/anger cartwheeling is definitely a challenge. Building your own strong, steady, loving relationship with your children will be important. It also helps if you aren't too needy yourself for the narcissist's attention and approval. When you can be strong enough to create structure, routine, and reliability in the face of the chaos that the narcissist creates, your children have a greater chance of stability and resilience.

Mistaken Goals

Children naturally try hard to learn how to belong and function in their family. They work to learn the rules and try to figure out how to successfully interact with their parents and later with the world. You can see their enthusiasm and determination as you watch them learn to walk, talk, feed, and dress themselves. They want to be like you. They want to feel competent and accepted.

But they can become discouraged when they can't find ways to please their parents and be warmly accepted and responded to. They want and need to have positive recognition, acknowledgment for their accomplishments, and encouragement for their individuality. As described above, these are the critical trust and safety deposits that are so often difficult for the NP/BP to do on a regular basis. When children can't successfully get their needs met or be accepted for their achievements, they'll try to find some other means to get their parent's attention and recognition.

Rudolph Dreikurs[5] identified four common "Mistaken Goals" that children often resort to when their basic emotional needs are hampered or lacking. They seek to belong through demanding *attention* or trying to over*power* the parent. If neither of these tactics works, they may move on to seeking *revenge* or collapsing into complete *inadequacy*. Because they so desperately want and need to make an emotional connection with their parents, children will usually keep trying, well into adulthood.

Seeking/Demanding Attention

When children can't get the positive attention they need from their parents, they'll sometimes increase attention-getting behaviors. They'll try bragging, showing off, clowning, interrupting, or become overly charming. If these more pleasing behaviors don't work, they'll move on to whining, demanding, petulance, and negative acting out. They will keep at it until they get your attention. If you've heard yourself saying, "Oh, he just wants attention," it may be that you have a child who is hungry to be seen, heard, and to belong to the family.

Children in NFS families often try to become the center of attention as a means to get their parents to stop fighting, or to soothe the atmosphere by taking your attention away from interactions that feel scary and alarming to them. A child who's in dire need of attention may end up never feeling like he/she measures up or belongs.

Giving your children appropriate and encouraging attention will do a lot to balance out the lack of positive attention and overly nega-tive attention from the NP/BP. You can easily become hyperfocused on the needs and demands of the self-absorbed parent and not notice your children languishing in the background. Children try hard to help their parents by being good, trying to learn, and struggling not to be a burden. But when they can't get appropriate attention and encourage-ment for their efforts, they will start doing more dramatic things to get their needs met.

Struggle for Power
It's been said that if you're fighting with your children to make them behave, you're in a lose-lose battle. Creating an atmosphere in which your children enjoy helping out, want to cooperate, and feel proud of what they can do for the family makes for a very positive parent/child relationship.

In the NFS family, children too often are the target of the NP/BP's overly zealous attention, anger, frustration, and blame. Children also tune in to the odd, unfair reversal that the NP/BP does when they ex-pect the children to behave more maturely and responsibly than they do. When children find themselves in an unfair, lose-lose situation, they're more likely to rebel. They may try to get you to see the unfair reality that permeates their interactions with the NP/BP parent, but that can leave you feeling split between siding with your partner-parent or your children. Throughout this book, we encourage you to think about siding with reality, sanity, and encouragement rather than the insanity, blame, and chaos created by the NP/BP parent.

Desire for Revenge
A child bent on revenge is a deeply discouraged child. He/she feels there is no hope of belonging through positive actions and feels it's impossible to win, so the next step is to make life miserable for parents and even for themselves. They may start stealing, flagrantly disobeying the rules, damaging the home, and acting out in the community. These

behaviors often signal that a child has essentially written off all hope of being seen, heard, or accepted by any other means. They take on the role of rebel, nonconformist, or agitator, mistakenly trying to assume the responsibility to dissent and revolt against the conditions they feel are overpowering their lives. They're sending the message that if the adults won't or can't stand up and change things, they'll do what they can to bring the problems to the surface.

A child who is willing to sacrifice himself to shine a light on the stress and problems in the family needs desperately to be heard. She/he is calling on you to be strong enough to take some kind of robust action to alter the family situation. Your children need to see that you have as much courage as they do to make things different.

Falling into Inadequacy
These children have given up. They've withdrawn, feel hopeless and helpless, see themselves as worthless, and feel unable to be successful by any means. They feel totally unable to meet their parents' expectations, and too inadequate to rebel. They've given up hope. The most they can usually do is passively defy you by not doing homework, not following through on responsibilities, and not finishing chores or else doing them poorly. They may cry and complain that they *can't* figure out what to do.

Many of these children are depressed, passive, and unfocused. They've lost hope that there is *any* solution to their being accepted or being able to contribute or help the family situation. These children are the ones most at risk for suicide or self-harm in the future. They need more than you can probably give them in your current family situation. They need counseling, tutoring help, and a way to find success—probably outside the family. For these children, it is often a long road to recovery.

Take Heart
Although you may feel discouraged and frightened about the impact the NP/BP may have on your children, we know there is a lot you can do to make life better for your children and ensure more positive outcomes for them. Remember, children are naturally very resilient. While children thrive more easily when both parents are well functioning, we

also know that even just one adult's positive support, love, strength, and moderating skills can hugely enhance a child's development and positive sense of self. You can do a lot to diminish the negative effect of the NP/BP's behaviors and teach your children what they need to learn to become well-adjusted, competent, loving people. In the coming chapters we'll help you fill your toolbox, and offer you the much-needed encouragement and support to give you the strength and courage to make important changes in your family life.

CHAPTER THREE

~

What the Narcissistic Family Is Like for You

Home Atmosphere

You know how intense and anxiety producing the atmosphere in your home can be. Sometimes the air feels like it could crackle with electricity. Other times it can feel empty and draining. Do you find yourself not wanting to go home or feeling more at ease when the NP/BP isn't there? Do you fear the drama or chaos you'll have to handle when he/she is around? It keeps you on edge wondering whether he/she will be in a good mood, happy, funny, full of life and energy, or pouting, hostile, attacking, or ominously quiet.

Unpredictable

Living in such an unpredictable atmosphere, your tendency is to either always be on guard, hypervigilant and tense, or go numb and move around in a daze of forgetfulness. It's exhausting to always be on guard, so as soon as the NP/BP acts normally, agreeable, and like the person you know and love, it's very easy to push the bad times into the back of your mind, forget they ever happened, and think to yourself that everything is better now and "back to normal."

Mystification

This forgetful state is called mystification, and it leads to you being surprised over and over when the other parent goes back to their self-involved, demanding, hostile, and blaming character again. This dazed fantasy of normality keeps you from being prepared for the next chaotic event, and can prevent you from problem solving how to handle it when it happens *again*. The confusing chaos that the NP/BP churns up and your own mystification make it hard for you to see the patterns in the NP/BP's behaviors or create strategies to challenge them.

Denial

Narcissistic and borderline traits don't magically heal themselves. NP/BPs consistently deny their own negative behaviors and blame others for their actions. Without taking responsibility for what they say and do, NP/BPs don't learn from their mistakes. They also don't believe or even adequately comprehend the emotional reactions of others to the hurtful, demeaning, and illogical things they say and do. So, again, they don't learn from seeing other's pain or hurt. In addition, whenever anyone gives into their selfish demands or puts up with their hostile, rude behaviors, the NP/BP is reinforced to continue behaving however they want again and again. So, when you go numb, forget the past, and assume things will just get better to ease the pain in the moment, it actually leads to increasingly worse behaviors by the NP/BP.

Hostility and Intimidation

When you point out, confront, or try to discuss problems, the NP/BP turns on you, attacks your shortcomings, and puts the blame on you. The NP/BP's response ends up making you feel ignored, discounted, or even made fun of. These attacks can quickly demolish your self-esteem and lead you to doubt your own feelings, observations, and sense of reality. Surprisingly, this can eventually lead you to trying harder and harder to please the NP/BP in order to get her/him to understand your perspective.

Accommodation

In order to calm the atmosphere, you have probably tried to be more kind and pleasing, give in to the NP/BP's demands and expectations, and even tried to see things from their perspective. However, these accommodations may have pulled you into joining with an irrational delusion that the NP/BP is right and reasonable and you're wrong and crazy. You can end up losing your own ability to see what is real, while it drains your strength and energy.

The Narcissistic/Borderline Partner

You find yourself always having to be on guard against the selfish, blameful, lack of respect, controlling, unreasonable, lack of empathy, and chaos that the NP/BP brings to your family life. They tell you they're being helpful and conscientious, and even brag they're doing everything while you do nothing. They strongly and emphatically assert that they are right and you're wrong. And they accuse you of all sorts of things that they actually do but you rarely or ever do. This can make you feel like you're crazy. Here are examples of common experiences.

Selfishness
People with narcissistic and borderline traits tend to be focused on their own needs, feelings, activities, and interests. Their actions are primarily prompted by these self-involved urges. For example, they say . . .

- I can't take the kids to soccer practice. My favorite show is on.
- I'm too tired and upset to deal with any of you.
- If you really cared about me, you'd keep the kids quiet.
- Dad, I want to go see the new movie. Honey, I know you'll love coming to watch me play baseball a lot more.
- Why don't you want to play the piano? I loved it as a kid.

They seem oblivious to their own self-serving expectations. However, they quickly blame you for being selfish if you ask for anything they don't want to provide or do.

Blaming
They blame others for their feelings and actions.

- You make me so mad.
- It's all because of you that I missed that deadline at work.

- You're just dawdling to try to make me late for my workout.
- Of course, I can't watch the children now. I'm too busy trying to take care of this family.
- You're all so selfish.

They can't see the negative effects of their own behaviors on others, but instantly attack you or the children for something they don't like. It leaves you feeling unfairly judged, misunderstood, and with a terrible urge to explain and have the truth acknowledged. But as much as you try, you can't get the NP/BP to see things from your perspective.

Lack of Respect
The NP/BP also doesn't have any sense of democracy or respect for the needs, opinions, or preferences of others.

- Of course, you'll love staying home with me today. Your friends are stupid anyway.
- You'll do it because I say so.
- Your mother agrees with me. You're going to do it the way I say.
- Sure, I told you that you could buy the shoes you wanted. But these are far better than the ones you picked out.

When your feelings, thoughts, and judgments are ignored, discounted, and rejected with no discussion, you feel unimportant, disregarded, and disrespected. Even when you bring it up to the NP/BP, they never seem to "get it" why you're reacting as you are. They assume their feelings and opinions would naturally be yours as well. When you disagree, they simply think you're wrong.

Controlling and Unreasonable
NP/BPs tend to use control, vague demands, and unreasonable punishments to control you and the children. To them, life is completely about what they're feeling at the moment. Especially when they feel anxious or insecure, they want to be in control of everything—whether it's time, money, attention, goals, interests, and more.

- I bought you that bike, and I can take it away if I want.
- You better make those kids clean their rooms, or I will absolutely not put up with it.

- You *will* finish that homework or you're not going to bed until you do.
- You better shape up, young lady, or you'll be grounded for the rest of your life.

You can end up feeling you have no voice and no power in your own home.

Self-Inflation
NP/BPs exaggerate their contribution to parenting, and constantly feel unappreciated.

- I do everything around here, and what do you do? Nothing.
- I work till I drop just to take care of all of you, and what thanks do I get?
- You are constantly giving in to those kids. I could make them obey, if you didn't sabotage me all the time.

You may see the NP/BP as being more difficult and troublesome than any of the children. You have to pick up after them, remind them of normal behaviors, deal with the emotional chaos they sow, and typically do most of the work that the home and family needs to function. The NP/BP's self-view is highly distorted, which can feel irksome and leaves you feeling unappreciated.

Lack of Empathy

The NP/BP can't recognize or comprehend others' feelings, so they're not capable of tuning into anyone else's needs. They're so engulfed with their own feelings and point of view that everyone else's become invisible to them. They see it as their job to make the rest of the family think and feel the same as they do. Basically, they function in their own world, which often doesn't emotionally include you.

This lack of empathy and understanding of how you feel leaves you with a sense of loneliness, emptiness, and isolation. You have probably dreamed of being close, supported, and working as partners in your life together. Without a sense of intimate connection, though, you and the children really exist in a world that has a separate existence from that of the NP/BP.

Chaos

It's all so confusing. When the NP/BP is in a good mood and doing things they enjoy, they can be delightful, fun, entertaining, and even considerate. Frequently, during those times, all the rules fly out the window. These on-again-off-again moods and behaviors throw everyone in the family off balance.

Expectations are frequently too high or too low. Family activities change at the last moment. No one gets a choice except the NP/BP. As a result, you may notice your children, and even yourself, lying, using manipulation, and even passive-aggressive behaviors to get your needs and wants satisfied. When it's impossible for anyone to get attention or other needs met directly, then trickery or acting out will develop and the Mistaken Goals mentioned in chapter 2 will appear. You'll find yourself always off balance, trying to soothe hurt feelings, striving to please everyone, but the result is that no one agrees on anything, feels safe, or gets their real needs met.

Tuned Out

The narcissistic/borderline parent doesn't seem to notice all the stress, anguish, and misery that you and the children are experiencing. When you finally convey that someone in the family is in pain or having difficulty, the NP/BP pretends that it'll go away on its own, that it isn't that bad, and if it is, it's all your fault. They label you as being the negative, pessimistic one of the family and themselves as the positive one. In actuality, the NP/BP is like a black hole of pessimism and criticism while claiming that everything in the family is just fine.

Can't Solve Problems

The NP/BP rarely participates in actually solving problems, but instead tries to find who to blame, doles out punishments, and frequently demands that no one outside the family should ever know about the issue. These are ways of avoiding awareness of problems in the family and continuing their belief that they have no issues themselves.

Because of the NP/BP's lack of understanding about feelings, lack of emotional bonding with others, and general misperceptions about how relationships function, they are really very poor at problem solving. They want you to provide answers that they can critique. But they really can't come up with solutions that work.

Too Much Caretaking

Overfunctioning

You've undoubtedly been struggling and trying to handle this chaos. It's probably clear to you that you're taking care of almost all of the responsibilities for the home, children, and family activities. In addition, you're trying to keep the NP/BP calm and unstressed so he/she doesn't create even more chaos and commotion. You find yourself always busy, rushing from one task to another, hardly having time to finish anything. It feels like you never have a moment to yourself. You're doing most of the parenting and working to keep your relationship together, while it often feels like the other parent is just a large, overdemanding, spoiled child that you also have to accommodate. You have no time to listen, plan, or stop to think.

Avoiding Conflict

To this point, you've been trying to do all this while also following the NP/BP's crazy expectations. You've been walking on eggshells to keep her/him happy. Most partners of NP/BPs don't like conflict, so you probably prefer to give in and give up rather than cause an argument or fight. And even when you do try to stand up for yourself or the children, you're faced with a barrage of multiple arguments that often don't make sense and are totally confusing. Trying to reason with the narcissistic/borderline parent seems to do no good. And even if you *win* your point and the other parent agrees to do something your way, it isn't long before he/she *forgets* or outright *denies* giving any approval.

Caretaker Role

You're in the role of the family caretaker.[1] You're caretaking the NP/BP, who is an adult and should be taking care of himself or herself. And you're caretaking the children who really do need your help. The one person in the family that you're not taking care of is yourself. This, of course, can lead to declining energy and increasing stress, anxiety, and even despair. You're living in a no-win situation for everyone but the narcissistic/borderline parent, who is demanding and getting what they want—despite thinking that they *never* get what they want and they're the most maligned person in the family. And it's always your job to fix everything.

Wishful Thinking Isn't the Same as Hope

You may try to keep yourself going with the fantasy that your partner will eventually see the light and come to understand how their behavior is hurting you and the children. You keep wishing they'll get better, come to their senses, start acting normally, or at least go to therapy. This feeds your need to keep up hope and not have to face the painful fact that your partner is severely emotionally disabled and won't ever be participating as you expected. Hope is based on real possibilities. However, the likelihood of the NP/BP seeing reality and responding as a true partner-parent is extremely low.

People Pleasing

It's almost inevitable that you'll find yourself going along with the NP/BP's demands and expectations. Pleasing the narcissist/borderline seems like the only way to keep the peace and keep the family functioning. It seems like the best choice in the short term. You may be too busy, too exhausted, and too overwhelmed to actually see the long-term costs of this choice.

You'll also get a lot of advice from the media, therapists, ministers, friends, and family. It's a common recommendation to put your energy into caretaking your partner and always keep up hope for the best. However, this advice assumes that you have a fully functioning partner who is reasonable, loving, and equally able and willing to care for you and participate in caring for the children. This, of course, is not the case in your situation. Trying to please and accommodate the NP/BP eventually places you and your children in emotional jeopardy.

Lack of Self Care

Caretakers eventually become discouraged, emotionally drained, and often physically ill. You're probably also working to keep yourself from falling into acute anxiety, depression, or hopelessness. In the NFS, you're under extreme pressure to make everything work out positively for everyone. This state of overfunctioning will eventually break down. It is much more common for the caretaking partner to enter therapy or be on antidepressants than for the NP/BP to seek help of any kind. "You're the one with the problem," they say. They think things are going quite fine for themselves just the way they are.

The narcissistic family system rarely feels at ease and comfortable. Even when things are going along fine, there's an uneasy feeling that something bad will happen if you're not paying close attention. Too often it feels chaotic and on the verge of collapse. You feel overwhelmed, distracted, and on edge. You try so hard to please everyone and make things work, but it rarely goes smoothly. Someone is always unhappy, distressed, or in conflict. Just when things settle down for a moment, another disaster happens, and you have to run to the rescue.

Your partner just doesn't seem to be able or willing to join in to solve problems or really connect with you and the children. His/her needs always seem to dominate your energy. You get things calmed down for a while, but another disaster always crops up. You feel like you're in a constant tightrope act. No matter what you try to fix, it never seems to be enough.

Learning to see the patterns that are operating in the NFS can help you see why things are constantly going awry. We'll look at those next.

CHAPTER FOUR

~

Narcissistic Family System
Patterns and Problems

Patterns and Problems

Every family evolves in unique ways; however, the narcissistic family system (NFS) consistently presents many common patterns. Naturally, not all of these patterns appear in every NFS, but you'll probably recognize quite a few. Learning to identify your family's particular patterns will help you know what new steps to take to change your interactions and create healthier responses in your family environment. Just stepping out of typical NFS behaviors can positively redirect the way you and your children respond to the world and feel about yourselves.

Keeping Up Appearances

Total Agreement
The NP/BP insists that the everyone in the family think, feel, choose, and act as identically as possible. Any disagreement with the NP/BP results in blowups and fights. So, you've probably learned to pretend that you agree, pretend that everything is OK, and pretend that you all feel alike. Pretending that everything is normal also protects your family image out in the community. Your united front keeps the hostile, angry, attacking, and belittling behaviors of your partner-parent hidden

from others, but it increases the isolation of your small nuclear family. In fact, your collusion of normality with your partner-parent may be the primary reason that your friends, family members, and community believe your family is happy and well-functioning.

Family Secrets

Keeping secrets is common in families with parental dysfunction. First of all, you're keeping the secret that the other parent is emotionally dysfunctional or even mentally ill. You probably have lots of ways of explaining their odd, angry, hurtful behaviors to your children and others—and even to yourself. You make excuses—for example, "He's had a bad day; She's on her period; He's depressed; She's really loving and caring most of the time; He's a good provider." You may also keep secret how much the other parent is drinking alcohol, using drugs—prescription or street drugs—gambling, or spending money recklessly. Even though you may fight with him or her about these things, you're still accepting and condoning these behaviors when you don't take action to protect yourself and your children.

The NP/BP may demand that certain topics be off limits to "outsiders" or insist that you not talk to particular friends or family members. This can result in hurt feelings and concerns from those friends and relatives. If and when they ask about what's going on, you may find yourself lying to keep the family secrets to the very people who could be your greatest source of support, help, encouragement, and validation.

Eventually, the NP/BP may even want you to cut off from your friends and even your family, especially if they're coaching you to leave, stand up for yourself, or get some kind of counseling. That's a huge threat for your partner who is very sensitive to being judged, abandoned, or seen as wrong or incompetent. The NP/BP will push hard to keep you away from people who might pull you out of relationship with her or him.

You won't have to explicitly tell your children to keep things secret. They'll know by how ashamed or angry you are, and they'll try hard to follow your example. When a family keeps secrets, it creates stress, anxiety, tension, and sometimes trauma for all family members, but especially the children.

Increasing Isolation

Eventually your family may become very isolated due to the mystification, secret keeping, and pretending to the outside world.[1] This causes stress, feeling on edge, depression, and shame. You may notice your children becoming angry, belligerent, withdrawn, and forgetful. Some children try, instead, to be more perfect, pleasing, and superachieving. Isolation makes it hard for your children to cope. When you pretend that everything's OK and act accepting of the hurtful and crazy behaviors of the other parent, your children are less and less likely to trust you or share their feelings and worries with you.

They probably won't talk to other adults either, because that would require them to be aware and acknowledge that things at home aren't normal. Talking to other adults would mean breaking the no-tattling rules *and* betraying their parents. It's highly unlikely.

You can be a powerful model and support to your children by keeping connections to positive, supportive people, staying active in the community, and giving them lots of opportunities to interact with other families, children, and healthy relatives. This may seem difficult, but it can make a world of difference to the well-being of your children, as well as yourself.

Poor Communication

Confusing Double-Talk

Double-talk means saying one thing but feeling or thinking another. You and your partner-parent may say things are "fine" when you're angry, or say "OK" even when you don't want to do something. You may be doing this to cover up unpleasant feelings or as a means to convey to each other that you're going along but protesting—depending on the way you change your voice inflection. Children are more adept at reading body language and voice tone than understanding words, so they'll pick up the underlying emotion and be confounded by the opposing mixture of words and feelings. Young children are confused by sarcasm, while older children will quickly learn to use it against you. Saying the opposite of what you want or feel creates unease, hypervigilance, and mistrust in children. They feel stupid, tricked, or even fearful when this happens a lot in the family.

Being direct and truthful can feel very vulnerable, but it will make communication more understandable for your children. It takes courage and persistence to make changes, but later chapters will give you some tools to help.

Not Listening

Hearing is not the same as listening. The narcissist/borderline may talk so much and with so little reality or logic, that you may just tune him/her out. You can end up tuning out your children as well, which leaves them isolated.

Learning to listen carefully for the underlying messages being sent by both the NP/BP and your children will help you get a better understanding of what your family members are really thinking and feeling. Really listening can do a lot to clear up much of the confusion going on in your family and help you figure out more effective responses.

Triangulation

Another common communication problem in NFS families is triangulation. That's where you send a message to someone through another person. For example, you're angry about something your partner-parent said or did and you complain about it to your children, instead of saying something directly to him/her. Or you talk about someone as if they aren't in the room. Or, your child wants to ask Dad for something but is afraid to ask and wants you to pass along the message instead.

As a result of these indirect communications, your children can get pulled into adult conflicts, and may even get the message that it's their job to make things better between you and the other parent. Directly communicating your thoughts, preferences, and decisions will help you move your whole family into more effective exchanges and provide a good model for your children as well.

Problems Don't Get Solved

A hallmark of the NFS is that problems never seem to get resolved, decisions aren't made, and solutions don't appear. Often when people are talking in the NFS, it's just a lot of words, off-topic comments, talking about others, and cutting remarks. Problem solving requires that issues be clear, feelings be heard but not expanded into drama, and solutions discussed calmly and logically. This is very difficult for the emotionally volatile parent to do. Logical problem solving can't get done unless all parties are able and willing to follow an orderly progression.

Old hurts, disappointments, emotional triggers, and resentments can also end up getting in the way of solving problems. For instance, a couple came to me years ago who couldn't get through any disagreement because the wife was still livid—after twenty-five years—that the husband hadn't been there for their first child's birth. He was angry at the unfairness of her accusation because he'd been deployed in Iraq at the time. These kinds of old hurts seem to never get resolved in NFS families and create mistrust and bitterness that can last for years.

Learning new ways to communicate that acknowledge the needs and feelings of everyone in the family can clarify the real issues and provide a healthy model for listening and responding that will be useful for your family.

Atmosphere

Fear, Obligation, Guilt

Randi Kreger, in her book *Stop Walking on Eggshells*, points out that NFS families are persistently filled with fear, obligation, and guilt.[2] These feelings get in the way of love, caring, intimacy, and tranquility. When you're afraid of oversized emotional outbursts, constantly prepared for chaos, and believe that you are responsible for everything that happens, then you're going to always be on guard, and you'll more likely make poor choices.

You may think that you have to do or say the exact right thing to keep things calm. Or, you may think you have to figure out how to fix or appease the narcissist/borderline parent's feelings, create secret solutions, and somehow figure out how to not upset him/her. This approach requires you to manipulate and control the NP/BP and your children rather than finding a real solution for what's happening.

When you're afraid, feel obligated to make the other person feel better, and don't believe in yourself, you'll feel powerless. Learning to change your own emotional responses and reactions to the narcissist/borderline can provide a model for your children. When you work on letting go of your fears and feelings of guilt for not being able to control or fix the NP/BP's emotional dysfunctions, then you can greatly change the atmosphere of your home life. It's amazing how you can then break through the status quo and change the conditions and ultimately the outcomes when you let go of your *fear*, *obligation*, and *guilt*.

Rarely Feels Safe and Comfortable

The actual air in your home can sometimes feel electric, oppressive, explosive, even when no one is saying anything. The NP/BP's volatile or negative energy seems to overtake everything. You read their emotions in their body language and facial expressions, even while the NP/BP is denying that anything is wrong. This uncertainty leaves everyone feeling constantly on guard, rarely relaxed or at ease, and emotionally and physically exhausted. What level of calm and comfort do you feel in your home? How often do you actually dread going home?

Creating soothing, safe spaces for your children and yourself will begin to create a different atmosphere. When you take better care of your own needs and emotions and are able to soothe and calm yourself, you will model these behaviors for your children. Removing yourself and your children from emotionally devastating and draining situations can also give your children a greater sense of protection and trust.

Under Siege

You may almost get a sense that you and your children are being held hostage in the distorted and bewildering delusional world of the NP/BP—and you are, if you believe what the NP/BP says is true. They can be so convinced that they're right, that their pronouncements are correct, and that they should be in control of everything, that you may start believing what they say as truth.

You are the sane, logical, competent parent, and you need to keep your strength and sanity at all times. Later chapters will show you how to be less anxious and use positive skills to sort through the chaos.

Perfectionism and Blame

The NP/BP demands perfection from others but doesn't seem to notice his/her own shortcomings. Anyone who doesn't match their exacting expectations will be shamed, blamed, and criticized. Too often family members expend a lot of energy trying to please the NP/BP—which is almost never successful anyway. Whether the narcissist/borderline is pleased or angry is entirely due to their mood at the moment. Buying into their perfectionism goal is a waste of energy and emotionally damaging. It can result in you and your children believing you aren't worthy of love or consideration unless you meet the NP/BP's perfectionistic standards. Don't believe or perpetuate the NP/BP's delusions. Instead, create your own atmosphere of truth, sanity, love, and caring with your children. Stay tuned into reality, be honest and genuine with them, and offer acceptance, support, love, and nurturing.

Family Divisions

Enmeshment and Power Conflicts

The NP/BP wants you to exactly match her/his emotions and thoughts. This is called *enmeshment*. They want you to merge your personality into theirs so you'll always think and feel exactly the same as they do. They view differences as meaning they're wrong, so they fight back against any variation they see from you or the children and demand that you see they are right.

So, to be yourself or to have an identity, you have to be in conflict with the narcissist/borderline. It's very likely that you deeply dislike conflict. Most people in long-term relationships with a narcissist/borderline tend to be easy-going, flexible, soothing, peacemakers. It's probably been quite shocking to you to be involved in so much conflict because the power struggles in this relationship seem endless and often happen about ridiculous things. The NP/BP blames you for these conflicts, but you probably notice that you have little or no fighting and discord with anyone else. Most of the conflicts in this relationship can come under one heading: the struggle by the narcissist/borderline to get you and the children to completely enmesh with him/her versus your struggle to keep your identity and sense of self.

Loyalty Demands

Not agreeing or doing exactly what the NP/BP wants is considered by them to be *disloyal*. They usually have rules about who you can talk to, what you can talk about, or where you can go and with whom. They may try to lure the children into liking them better and even disliking or disregarding you. They may try to undermine your parental authority by encouraging the children to break the rules or keep secrets from you, or they demean you in front of the children. The message is that you're either on their side or you're the enemy.

Lack of Unity
Because of these distortions, polarized thinking, and the power struggles for dominance and individuality, your family always seems to be taking sides against one another, rather than working together. There really is no lasting unity. The family can seem like an arena of individual gladiators fighting each other rather than working toward a common goal. The NFS can't function as a unified force because the narcissist/borderline is so fully controlled by his/her emotional disabilities and lack of reality, and you're exhausted with the chaos and confusion.

Loss of Community Supports
Over time you'll find you have fewer and fewer friends and that you're probably losing contact with your family. The NP/BP may want you to work from home, stay home from work, or even quit your job. You or the other parent may consider homeschooling as a way to deal with your children acting out or to keep them from getting negative school reports. The NP/BP may start cutting you off from community activities, church and social events, going to the gym, or even going shopping by controlling the money or being critical and dismissive of your choices. These even further isolate you.

Agreeing to these demands means that you and your children will have fewer and fewer supports. You then have no one to keep you on track and point out when your beliefs and assumptions are getting out of whack. And you have no one to confide in or help you care for your children. This will cut your children off even further from information, feedback, and the support of sane, kind, and helpful people.

Nigella
My husband, Jerry, who is very religious, agreed we could go to the church pastor for counseling. However, when the pastor started suggesting that Jerry should talk kindly instead of angrily to me and the children, and consider his contribution to our problems, Jerry refused to

go back. Not just to the counseling, but to the church. So, he started a Bible study group in our home with five other people. Now that group has even disbanded. I can't go alone to church because Jerry would think that was disloyal of me. I really miss our friends and the community activities. It's just Jerry, the kids, and me these days.

Do everything you can to keep your children connected with community support systems—schools, sports, group activities, teachers, events with other families, and more. Encourage them to join in, go to friends' homes, learn new skills, participate on teams, get a job, or volunteer to help others. The more time they spend outside the home in supportive and rewarding experiences with other healthy people, the less impactful the behaviors of the unstable parent will have on them.

Getting Professional Help

Getting really useful professional counseling can be a complicated process for an NFS family. Your emotionally unstable partner-parent is unlikely to want you to take your children to counseling or to go with you to couple's or family counseling. They're too afraid of being identified as having a problem, feeling judged, or being blamed—none of which they would be able to tolerate. They may go for a session or two, but typically will leave in an angry outburst the minute the counselor implies they have any responsibility for the problems that you're there to work on. The NP/BP may also pressure you to stop counseling, refuse to pay for the help, and be totally uncooperative.

If you go to a family therapist, she or he is likely to want all of you to come into the session. In families like yours, your children probably won't want to open up about what's going on unless you do. However, if you start being critical of the NP/BP parent, he/she will probably attack you either in the session or afterward at home. This puts you into a lose-lose situation.

People with narcissist/borderline traits are hard to spot in therapy because they're really good at looking like the aggrieved party. They say they don't have any problems and you're always complaining. So, if you don't clearly clue-in the therapist about the severe emotional instability of the other parent, you'll end up being the focus of more criticism and attacks from the NP/BP in the therapy session or afterward. On the other hand, many therapists are suspicious of any pre-session information or any negative comments about the other parent.[3]

Most therapists have had little or no training to deal with a couple when one has narcissistic/borderline personality traits. As a result, many of the suggestions and directions you'll get from these therapy sessions will be unhelpful and may actually be damaging. Most couple's therapy will focus on the two of you "communicating better, sharing your feelings, and paying more attention to each other." These suggestions can easily be used by the NP/BP to demand more and more agreement and attention from you, which can make your relationship worse for you while not making any changes in your dysfunctional family system.

If you go to see your pastor or priest for help, things could go even more off track. People with narcissistic/borderline traits try very hard to appear normal, reasonable, and nice in a session with someone they really want to please. And people in the clergy are also not well trained to counsel people with borderline or narcissistic problems. Platitudes and more love don't cure mental illness. When the emotional instability of a parent isn't directly addressed, the parenting suggestions you're given—however good they may be for a normal family—can end up coming to failure and disappointment for you and your children.

Every NFS family is complicated, and the patterns and rules end up being debilitating to the emotional health and well-being of all the family members. If you want to change what is going on in your family, then you can't wait for the NP/BP parent to lead the way, give you permission, or somehow magically heal themselves.

Your first step in creating a better family life for your children is learning to recognize the dysfunctional patterns that are happening in your particular family. The NP/BP's behaviors can seem confusing and may seem random, but you'll see clear patterns, when you look for them.

To move out of these patterns, you have to accept that: 1) your partner-parent is emotionally unstable, 2) he/she is majorly self-absorbed in their own pain and fantasies, and 3) none of their character traits or behaviors are likely to change anytime soon. When you see these facts clearly, then you will find yourself on a different playing field. You will no longer keep expecting him/her to act *normally*. You will be less often thrown off track or confused about what is going on. You can then anticipate the NP/BP's emotionally out-of-sync reactions, and you can be prepared to respond more effectively.

The rest of this book offers information on how to build up your own and your children's resilience, learn new ways to respond to these family problems, and deliver more effective outcomes for yourself and your children. We will help you change your focus from trying to fix, heal, and accommodate the NP/BP—which is not working—to focusing on increasing your own emotional strength and self-care so that you can give your children the hope, resources, and love that will help them develop into the strong, competent, healthy individuals you wish them to be.

PART II

BUILDING RESILIENCE

CHAPTER FIVE

~

Resilient Parent, Resilient Child

Resilience is the ability to bounce back from stress, challenge, tragedy, trauma, or adversity. It is one of the most effective tools you will ever place in your parenting toolkit to help your children. Resilience is about being flexible in your thoughts and actions even through adverse or challenging experiences. Like it or not, adversity and challenge are part of our human condition.

You can't always control what happens in life. And you certainly can't control all of the things the other parent or people outside the family might say or do. Much as you'd like to encase your children in bubble wrap to protect them from every bad thing that might happen to them, it's simply not possible. What you can do is help them learn to use a variety of skills and cultivate a way of thinking that will prepare them for the many emotional and physical challenges they'll meet in life. In other words, you can teach your children to be resilient.

Recent advances in neuroscience have given us valuable information about how we learn to be resilient. While some resilience strategies may initially seem like nothing more than common sense, it turns out each resilience-building strategy is solidly backed by extensive research. In the upcoming chapters we will present a number of these strategies to support and help you be emotionally available and responsive to your children's needs. These resilience-building experiences will help you teach and model effective coping strategies.

It may feel like an overwhelming task with a narcissistic/borderline parenting partner to also put extra thought and planning into what you teach your children. But take heart, because you can do this. Resilience is built through small actions done frequently. Before we get into specific strategies, let's look at a brief overview of what we mean by resilience.

Components of Resilience

Resilience is a combination of actions and mindset. Resilient children (or adults) employ many different skills to help themselves recover from the disappointments and challenges that come their way. Over time you learn to have a positive mindset that helps you bounce back from difficult experiences. It's a way of thinking that contributes to a positive frame of mind, instead of getting stuck or feeling like a victim to the situation or a controlling person. Therapist and author Bonnie Badenoch, PhD[1] calls this getting-stuck feeling "neural cement." Resilience helps us steer clear. Here's an example:

Micah

Eight-year-old Micah was looking forward to spending the day with his grandparents. They'd planned to go to his favorite minigolf course in a nearby town. When the day arrived, Micah showed up in shorts and hat, eager for a day of minigolf and fun. Unfortunately, the day before, the grandparents' car had developed a problematic clunking sound and they were reluctant to take it on the road. They told Micah they wouldn't be able to go to the minigolf course because of the car, and then described a new plan for several fun activities that were in town. Understandably, his first reaction was disappointment. His eyes filled with tears, his shoulders slumped, and his face seemed to cloud over. His grandparents allowed him to fully feel his disappointment instead of trying to talk him out of it. "I know you were really looking forward to playing minigolf today," his grandmother said. "It's hard to accept when things don't work out as we plan." Micah nodded. After a couple of minutes, he said, "So we're going to the trampoline place and then we'll have a picnic at the park?" He took a breath, his shoulders relaxing. "Well that sounds like a fun day. Maybe we can go to the golf place another day." His grandparents agreed.

Micah didn't get stuck in neural cement. The adults acknowledged his disappointment and gave him time to work through it. Because this resilient behavior had already been modeled for him many times in his life, he was able to adjust and move on. He was growing his own set of coping skills to use when his plans didn't work out.

Attributes of Resilient People
People who are resilient share a set of abilities that help them get through challenging situations. They include:

- A *strong problem-solving approach to challenges*. They see difficult situations as something to be solved rather than frightening and overwhelming.
- *The ability to reframe disappointment and manage emotions*. Instead of experiencing an event as a disaster, they see it as a disappointment and search for another alternative.
- *Self-confidence*. Resilient people know that solutions are dependent on what they do rather than hoping others will change.
- A *strong moral compass*. They look to their own values and ethics as guidelines for their choices.
- A *sense of humor*. They accept situations for what they are, so they can see the whole picture—even the irony and humor.
- A *willingness to ask for and receive help* when needed. They don't expect to know or be able to handle everything on their own. They feel deserving of support.
- *Independence paired with healthy connections to others*. They trust their own judgment and make considered choices with helpful input from a trusted and caring support group.

In the following chapters we'll be describing these skills and how to increase them in yourself and your children.

Conditioning and Neuroplasticity
Two important aspects of brain functioning are particularly relevant to developing resilience. The first is *conditioning*—that is, how you

initially encode events in your brain. This is where early relationship experiences come into play. Human beings learn in social contexts. Interactions with parents and/or caregivers set the stage for numerous important neurological developments. Babies learn to feel trust and safety in their environment when they get their important needs met.

Children gain the underpinnings of self-worth from their day-to-day interactions with all the adults around them. When a parent models trust, self-acceptance, and calm coping behaviors, it supports healthy brain development and gives children an important head start in developing resilience.

The second important aspect of brain functioning is *neuroplasticity*—which is the mechanism that allows brains to grow and rewire through new experiences. Neuroplasticity means that the brain is continually adapting and changing due to your everyday experiences and what those experiences mean to you. With each new experience, you have a chance to encourage positive changes in the brain by how you interpret those experiences, whereas negative interpretations can create rigidity, fear, and stress.

That means the ability to change, grow, and become stronger exists throughout our lives. Even when a person has a less-than-ideal early beginning, thanks to neuroplasticity, they can still develop healthy coping skills and a positive frame of mind through new information and understanding.

Interruptions to Developing Resilience

There are four big early life events that can affect brain development and interrupt a child's ability to cope with life stressors and develop resilience.

Attachment Issues

When something happens early on that interferes with an infant's ability to bond with a primary caregiver, the brain's resources tend to focus on survival rather than brain development. Any number of events can interrupt healthy attachment. For example, mental or physical illness in a parent, physical challenges or illness in the child, maternal stress or fatigue, parental substance abuse, physical abuse, sexual abuse, neglect, being put up for adoption, or the death of a parent. Any of these can contribute to problems in attachment.

Poor Resilience Skills in Parents or Caregivers
When parents or caregivers have not developed their own resilience skills, they'll be unable to model this for their children. Parents with narcissistic or borderline disabilities are often unable to be resilient in difficult situations due to their own emotional fears, stresses, rigid rules, and emotional upheavals. This can increase their children's anxieties and negative reactions to adverse situations.

Adverse Childhood Experiences
The Substance Abuse and Mental Health Services Administration or SAMHSA[2] defines Adverse Childhood Experiences (ACEs) as stressful or traumatic events, including abuse and neglect, household dysfunction, witnessing domestic violence, or living with family members who have substance use disorders. These ACEs are very likely to negatively affect brain development and resilience. The erratic and suddenly emotionally charged reactions of a narcissist/borderline parent are adverse situations that are hard for children to understand and know how to respond to.

Acute Trauma in Childhood
There are a number of traumatic events that are largely outside a parent's control and can have negative consequences for healthy brain development—living through a natural disaster like a hurricane or flood, the death of a loved one, a serious illness of the child or a significant caregiver, having a parent with mental illness, losing a home, or having a parent in prison. These traumatic events can seriously disrupt the normal developmental stages of brain growth. The magnitude of these events is simply overwhelming to children. Instead of developing flexibility and resilience, their energy is devoted to survival.

With each of these potential interruptions to healthy brain development, there are actions that can be taken to turn them around. With some work and determination, a child's initial response and interpretation of an acute experience can be modified and refashioned into a learning experience. Supportive adults can help a child transform a confusing, hurtful event into a learning situation that can build self-confidence, flexibility, and resilience. Neuroplasticity saves the day here.

You Can Make a Difference

You are the most important factor in helping your children develop resilience. Human brains learn through social interactions. Positive interactions build resilience, even when you're also exposed to negative situations and people. How you pay attention to your children, how you explain events, and how you react to adversity can provide powerful skills and examples for your children to learn to be resilient. Interestingly, resilience is like a circle. Each time you help your children be more resilient, you strengthen your own resilience.

Author and family therapist Linda Graham writes extensively about resilience. In her book *Bouncing Back*,[3] she presents the Five Cs of Resilient Coping that help to rewire old dysfunctional patterns of behavior and build new neural circuitry to increase resilience. They are:

- learning to remain *calm* in a crisis
- developing *clarity* to see your internal reactions to an experience as well as to clearly see the experience for what it is
- *connection* to loving, supportive people who offer resources and help when needed, and model healthy resilience
- using previously learned skills and *competencies* to enable quick and effective action to stresses and challenges
- drawing on *courage* to persevere, bounce back, and find resolution or acceptance to stressful events

Think of resilience as a muscle. The more you use it, the stronger it becomes. As you employ calmness, clarity, connection, competence, and courage when faced with challenges, disappointments, and difficult experiences, you model resilience for your children. And you strengthen your own resilience.

Every person and every family faces difficulties and challenges day by day and throughout life. Early traumas and adversities can have a damaging effect on the development of the brain and personality. However, brains have the ability to change and evolve when the individual has a willingness to learn and positive teachers and role models. The earlier children feel a sense of love, security, and positive, nurturing responses from their parents and other adults, the more they'll be able to develop resilience, emotional strength, and hardiness of spirit. Even when one parent is unstable and lacks adaptability, the other adults in the child's life can do a great deal to compensate for those deficiencies through modeling, positive attention, and reality-based feedback. You can help your children develop more resilience, and at the same time increase your own ability to respond to difficulties.

The next several chapters explain the unique complexities and challenges of sharing parenting with a partner who has narcissistic or borderline traits and behaviors. We outline these carefully, so that in later chapters we can identify the skills and strategies that you can use to teach and model for your children ways that help them develop greater self-compassion, competence, self-confidence, and resilience.

~

CHAPTER SIX

Changing Directions

The way your family system currently functions is probably quite variable day to day—often depending on the moods and behaviors of the NP/BP. This can leave you and the children always on guard for the next big explosion, sudden change in plans, or drama that needs handling. We know, however, there are strategies you can learn to use that will change the atmosphere of your home, improve your communication with your children, help them understand with compassion, and give them the tools they need to be successful in their adult relationships.

In order to help your children, you'll have to learn to trust your own judgments and keep tightly focused on reality. You won't need to spend your energy on trying to change the NP/BP. You'll be changing the direction of your attention. Instead of always taking care of the NP/BP's wants and demands, you'll be focusing on your relationship with your children. Making yourself and your children your top priority will make a world of difference.

Finding and Facing Truth

You don't have to have a psychiatrist give your partner-parent a formal diagnosis in order to know what the truth is. If he or she shows the patterns and behaviors that we've outlined, over a period of time, if the two of you rarely find solutions to your problems, if you're frequently shocked, irritated, and feel crazy around your partner-parent, and if your self-esteem and self-confidence feel eroded when you're around him/her, then you're parenting with an impaired partner who has a personality disorder.

Facing the truth of your partner-parent's disability is the first step in changing your life and your children's lives. This awareness can be scary, hard to understand, disappointing, overwhelming, angering, and maybe also relieving. In order to make changes that really work, you'll have to know and accept the truth of the situation that you're confronting.

Letting yourself take in the whole picture, instead of just what fits your hopes and dreams, can be earthshaking. At the deepest level, it shatters the dream you've had about your partner, your relationship, and even your future. You aren't parenting with an obstinate, confused, difficult person who just needs more information and rational advice. You're parenting with a person who has serious emotional deficiencies that you cannot alter or change.

Yes, he/she also has many positive qualities, but you can no longer forget that this is a person who will always have distorted beliefs, dysregulated emotions, and be extremely focused on their own needs and wants. He/she will continue to show abnormal reactions no matter what you say or do. Coming to this awareness, however, will help eliminate your constant need to make the NP/BP understand what's wrong with their behavior, or try to get her/him to change. You'll be better able to predict and respond to their odd and unsociable reactions to events. And it'll be easier to not take what they say and do personally.

On the other hand, you may now find yourself with a whole new set of fears and questions: What's wrong with me that I chose this person? How can I cope with this? What does this mean for my life? Will the NP/BP damage the children? How could I have put my children in this situation?

These fear thoughts won't help you cope. Neither you nor your partner-parent have done anything stupid or wrong. You're just seeing the situation more clearly, and it's not what you expected. It definitely requires a change of direction and a change of plans. So, breathe, let your fears settle, and realize that nothing has actually changed—except now you know what's going on.

Gather Your Strength and Resources

Where do you find strength? What helps you feel stronger? Do you have friends and close family to give you courage? Do you find your spiritual practices reinforcing? Do you need professional support and advice from a counselor, a financial advisor, and/or a legal expert? Do you need to increase your self-care? Most people who realize they're in this situation need all of these things to cope. So, gather your resources, collect as much information as you can, but most importantly be good to yourself. Talk to yourself in encouraging ways. Give yourself credit for your talents and abilities. Get enough sleep, eat well, and exercise. You've been taking care of your partner-parent's needs and wants to the detriment of your own. Now you need to take care of yourself so you can decide rationally what will be your best steps forward.

Facing Your Own Emotional Damage

When you face a new and perhaps startling truth and it rocks your world, all sorts of things happen in your mind, body, and emotional systems. They are all thrown out of kilter. They all have to adjust to this new information. Your partner is unable to function the way you thought he/she could. Your expectations are disrupted and spoiled. The dream you had of your life is fragmented. The way you thought your life would unfold has collapsed. The person you thought was going to be your partner, your closest supporter, and who was going to help you with the challenges of life won't ever be able to function in the way you expected.

Give yourself time to make these mental and emotional adjustments. Let this new information work itself through possible new scenarios in your mind. But beware of your own scare tactics. The brain is designed to react instantaneously to threat by fighting, fleeing, or freezing. *None* of these responses will help you with this situation. In fact, you have to let those reactions flow in, through, and out of your mind before you can actually start thinking of what you really want to do next. This takes time. So, don't make any sudden changes or decisions until your mind settles down again.

The other thing your brain will do during this time is bring up every pain, disappointment, wrong choice, shameful, fearful, and traumatic event you have ever experienced. Your brain is actually trying to help you prepare by going over these events so you can glean from them any insight about how to handle this new situation. It's a primitive reaction that worked when we lived in the wilds and our only choices were to run, hide, or defend. Now, however, we've evolved so quickly into a relationship society that this reaction of the brain isn't very helpful anymore. This painful review is not going to help because there are now millions of choices and you've never been who you are NOW, in the situation you're in NOW.

If you had a parent who had narcissistic or borderline behaviors, you may be having an even stronger reaction. If you weren't protected well as a child, if you weren't taught to be assertive or speak up for yourself, if you were punished for being imperfect, or your needs and wants were disregarded, this awareness that you're back in the same situation can be especially distressing. However, as an adult you now have the power to make your own decisions, learn new ways to protect yourself, and change the past story of your life. And you have the power to write a different story for your children.

Now is the time to get whatever help you need to work through any old hurts that come up. It's time to gather your strength to care for yourself and your children. It's time to formulate a new plan for your life. I once heard someone say, "Living well in the present is the best revenge for a difficult past." Living NOW always overrides living in the past. Let this experience today give you the motivation to move above and beyond the hurts of the past and overcome your fears. You have a right to pursue happiness and to make the changes necessary to live a better life.

Let Go of Shame and Guilt

Most of us aren't in touch with our sense of shame. It's almost as if we're actually ashamed of feeling shame. It's much easier to talk about self-esteem, identity, and strengths. However, you can only build yourself up by first letting go of those things that hold you back.

Shame is a dread of rejection and criticism of *who you are*. This is a core human fear. Humans can't survive entirely alone, so our emotional system is quite attuned to the threat of being cast out of any close relationship. The NP/BP sends out lots of shame messages and puts them on you. It's a way to rid themselves of feelings they can't stand.

Guilt is a feeling of responsibility for hurting others. Real guilt comes when you've actually been the cause of hurting someone. It's a common pattern for NP/BPs to say and do things that increase your shame and guilt. They blame you for not being perfect, not being able to make them happy, being too negative, being too needy, and being selfish. They believe that *you* cause their unhappiness. They can't see that it's the result of their own dysfunctional emotional system.

Letting go of these guilt-producing messages will go a long way toward improving your sense of well-being, self-compassion, and self-confidence.

- *Not Being Perfect.* Of course, you're not perfect. Nor should you expect yourself to be. NOBODY is perfect. Being loving and kind to yourself when you make mistakes or when things don't go as planned are good ways to move shame out of your life.
- *Not Making the Narcissist/Borderline Happy.* Even the NP/BP can't make themselves happy, so what chance do you have? We are each responsible to make ourselves happy.
- *Being Too Negative.* The fact that you don't like being treated with disdain, ignored, insulted, or blamed unfairly doesn't mean that you're being negative. No one likes feeling those things.
- *Being Too Needy.* As humans we live in groups and form relationships because we can't survive alone, and we are always in need of help. When you're ashamed of your needs and feel undeserving, the NP/BP can pressure you into spending all of your time and energy on them. It's OK to need love and care from others. It is not weak or self-centered to want to be loved, cared for, and treated with compassion. It is perfectly, humanly normal.

- *Being Selfish.* Taking care of your own needs is NOT selfish. In fact, your number-one job in life is to take care of yourself. Don't let yourself be blackmailed into giving up your own primary needs to make someone else happy just because they might think you're selfish.

Shame and guilt can be reinforced by others. However, the real source of the most hurt from shame or guilt is inside ourselves in the form of self-criticism and feeling unworthy. Self-compassion helps to neutralize shame. Talking to yourself with loving kindness, acceptance, and understanding is the best ways to replace shame and guilt. How would you talk to a friend or a child who is fearful, hurt, and worried? Talk to yourself in the same way.

It takes practice to change the habit of self-criticism. When you accept your own human needs, stop expecting yourself to be perfect, and tamp down your self-criticism, you'll have more energy to take loving care of yourself and your children. When you don't buy in to the belief that you're the cause of the NP/BP's pain, then their demands to give up your life for what they want and their threats and intimidation using shame and guilt won't have the hurtful impact they have had in the past.

Loving Self-Acceptance

Surprisingly the fastest way to heal old hurts, mistakes, and misjudgments is through self-acceptance.[1] Human beings are actually not motivated by criticism or rejection. We're much more likely to change when we feel acceptance and support, and when we see things as they are. You've been hoping to get understanding and truthfulness from your partner, but what you really need is to give those things to yourself. When you see and accept the truth of your family situation, coupled with a loving acceptance of yourself, you'll find it easier to make healthier choices. You'll also be more able to see the realistic available options while feeling far less fear and intimidation.

When you see, know, believe in, and accept yourself just as you are, your life will reflect a whole new level of wisdom, authenticity, and genuineness. You'll be able to see the truth about yourself that no one else can control or distort. When you know and lovingly accept yourself, you'll be less vulnerable to pressure from others to act against your own well-being.

Help to Let Go of Fear

All your self-criticisms, need to please, and anxiety about what's going to happen next are based in fear. That fear has been built up by a core belief that you have to please others, change yourself for them, and do what they want or you'll be abandoned and die. This is an ancient gut reaction based on being shunned from the tribe. You're not in that situation today, but the reaction may still be there in your body. When you lovingly accept yourself, the need to be and do what others demand dissolves into the background. However, as noted previously, when big changes are happening, whatever fears you already have will come to the surface.

Fear is our normal and natural reaction to danger. When humans were facing down lions and tigers, our bodies would pull all our blood and energy into our core so we'd have the energy to run. In threatening relationship situations today, our bodies still react the same way, giving us intestinal cramping, rapid heartbeats, sweating, and an inability to think clearly. We have to override these fear responses or give them time to pass in order to make clear judgments.

So, in order to let go of fear, you will first have to get your breathing under control. Taking deep, slow breaths will slow down your heart rate, relax your muscles, and allow blood to flow back into your brain. Imagine breathing out your fear, and breathing in safety and relaxation. Do this for several minutes, until you notice your body relaxing.

Thoughts are also an excellent way to challenge imagined fears. Ask yourself: "Am I in actual danger in this moment?" If you are, leave the situation immediately. If you really aren't in imminent danger, identify a statement that brings you a feeling of comfort and acceptance, such as:

- I am safe.
- I am able to handle what is happening.

- I know who I am.
- I have the right to have my own thoughts and feelings.
- I don't have to agree with anyone else.
- I choose my own way.
- I am brave and strong.
- I believe in myself.

Keep practicing your calm breathing and encouraging thoughts until they're second nature to you. For years I (Margalis) wore a bracelet inscribed with the phrase, "To thine own self be true." It got me through a lot of scary interactions. Fears don't go away instantly, but as you move yourself more and more into accepting yourself in the present moment and believing in your own self-worth, your fears become more manageable.

Help to Heal Your Grief
Undoubtedly grief will also surface as you face the reality of your relationship and family situation. Grief can appear in many ways through anger, bargaining, despair, depression, withdrawal, and even a deep level of exhaustion. You may sometimes feel hopeless and helpless. These reactions indicate your emotional system is coming to terms with the reality that your hopes, dreams, and expectations will not happen the way you wanted. True acceptance often brings with it feelings of grief over this loss.

When one dream is gone, it helps to find another dream just as worthy and engaging. That may seem impossible right now, but you and your children have the rest of your lives full of choices and new opportunities to pull you forward when you're ready. You had hoped for a cooperative, supportive, accepting relationship with your partner-parent. There may be a lot of inadequacies in achieving that with the NP/BP, but you can turn your attention toward being cooperative, supportive, and accepting in your relationship with your children.

You can create healthy communication, a loving atmosphere, a safe setting for exchanging feelings, and an environment of truth and directness between you and your children. You can create a parent-child relationship where you and your children can thrive, where you have trust and a deep sense of connection. Seeing your children grow into self-assured, competent, warm, loving adults can fulfill many of your hopes and dreams.

It's the nature of life to ebb and flow, have growing seasons and fallow times, to be exuberant and to rest. Life really is a cycle of complements. Healing is a time of internal adjustment. Loving self-acceptance during this time will help you get through it to the next phase—whatever you decide that will be.

Becoming a Warrior

When you're ready, you'll feel an increase in your energy. New ideas and ways of looking at things will appear. You'll feel a stirring of wanting to take action—not out of desperation, but from a sense of being ready to move on. Loving self-acceptance can turn your hurt, grief, and loss into determination to create something better for yourself and your children. It may take you a few days, weeks, or months of healing. You'll need support from others, lots of sleep, therapy, prayer, running and pushups, talking, thinking, planning, rewriting your life script, or whatever works for you. Eventually you'll start feeling differently about yourself and your situation. You'll have new ideas, and your determination will start growing to do something about them.

Becoming a warrior means you define your goal, gather your strengths, build up your courage, take a stand, and take new steps to move forward. You're about to change your life and your children's future for the better. Remember the movie where Wonder Woman charges across that field, fending off bullets, with every ounce of courage and strength she had? Whether you're male or female, that determination to reach your goal will keep you moving forward until you reach it. Your goal now is primarily to create a healthier, more loving, and nurturing life for your children and yourself. You can't force your NP/BP partner to come along. He or she may make changes to fit in better, or not. In either case, with courage, determination, and new insights and skills you can, and will, reach your goal. That's what a warrior does.

You can become a strong model, coach, and supporter of your children's growth and healthy development. You and your children can make changes that can heal the pain you've felt in this relationship. It will sometimes be scary and uncertain, but look at how much you have to gain. The following chapters will give you ideas, skills, and techniques to help you build resilience in yourself and your children.

CHAPTER SEVEN

Building Your Own Resilience

Having an emotionally impaired partner-parent is a big challenge in itself. Realizing that much of the resilience that your children develop is going to be almost entirely up to you to teach them is an additional challenge. However, it's a challenge that will increase resilience in you as well as your children. You are your children's greatest role model. Therefore, building up your own resilience will provide them with the example they'll need to gain their own emotional strength.

Preparing Yourself

No doubt about it, if you want to help your children develop into strong, independent, capable, and emotionally healthy individuals, you'll have to be strong as well. You'll need a clear picture of the kind of parenting you want to do and have the courage and determination to follow through with your plan. You'll need support from others, and you'll need to stay healthy both physically and emotionally. Here are our suggestions about how to do that.

Tune into Yourself

Too much of your time and energy has been spent attending to the needs, moods, demands, and emotional cycles of the NP/BP. This has taken your attention away from where it needs to be—paying attention to your own feelings and needs and those of your children. Any time you turn your attention away from the NP/BP you've been accused of being selfish, so you may have gotten into the habit of not thinking about what you feel or want. But it's time now to refocus on yourself.

To develop resilience, you have to know what you really feel, what is important to you, and what you value. Resilience is the ability to head in the direction that is right for you and to be able to bounce back when you confront obstacles. You also need to know what you feel and want in the moment so you can choose what action will best suit the situation. In addition, when you clearly know your own deeply held principles, values, and intentions, you can keep your personal compass to your true North.

Tuning into what you feel may be challenging at first. Try looking at a list of feeling words. See Appendix A. Several times a day, try to identify at least three or four that describe what you're experiencing right at that moment.[1] You'll notice that you usually have several feelings at once, and they may not all seem alike. That's normal. You may also notice that you and the NP/BP almost never feel the same thing at the same time. That's also normal. Keep practicing. Knowing what you feel will help you tremendously in figuring out what actions you want to take, rather than just going along with whatever the NP/BP wants.

Change Your Thinking

You have undoubtedly spent most of your attention in this relationship on trying to caretake, calm, and placate your partner-parent. The NP/BP's needs and demands have dominated and taken precedence. Common marital advice these days is that you should create a strong couple bond as the foundation for positive parenting and good family relationships. However, the relationship atmosphere with a narcissist/borderline partner is highly random, uncontrollable, and often negative. There's little you can to do to increase your partner's mental health.

So, we're suggesting that you focus, instead, on creating a strong, positive bond between your children and yourself. Instead of trying to fix, change, or control your partner-parent, put your concentration and attention on encouraging, inspiring, and fostering resilience, confidence, and positive mental health in your children and yourself.

You don't have to get the narcissist/borderline parent's permission, or convert or change him/her in any way to make this happen. You can just start doing it. If you have a good bond, determination, courage, and a plan, you will have a great amount of influence on your children's emotional well-being.

Determination

Determination is key. It includes purpose, resolve, and grit. Changing your purpose from appeasing, pleasing, and caretaking your partner-parent to being a strong, resilient parent helps you set that determination. You're now directing your energy into creating an atmosphere of love, caring, and primary responsiveness to your children. Resolving to keep your attention on your parent-child relationship gives you momentum to keep moving in the direction that you've chosen. And it keeps you from getting hooked into useless, unproductive, circuitous interactions with the NP/BP.

Emotional Insulation

Developing emotional insulation will benefit you greatly in all your interactions with the narcissist/borderline. He/she grabs your attention and pulls you into arguments by saying and doing things that will activate your emotional triggers. These can include bringing up your fears, insulting or belittling you, disparaging your children, criticizing your competence, mocking, ridicule, and more. Emotional insulation is an internal boundary that prevents these hostile and wounding comments and actions from making such a hurtful impact. If you aren't emotionally insulated, you'll get pulled into the craziness, become distracted, and make mistaken responses.

To insulate yourself, you'll need to be aware that when the NP/BP is saying or doing these insulting and hurtful things, he/she is incapable of being rational at that time. This is an alert that you need to protect yourself and your children. Learning to not take anything the NP/BP says or does personally is the best emotional insulation.

It's totally natural to want your partner-parent to love and respect you, but when they're in that irrational and senseless state of mind, it's not possible for them to do that. You must not buy into their insanity by thinking that what they're saying and doing makes sense, nor should you take it to heart. It is very important to NOT engage with the NP/BP when they are in an irrational state of mind. Arguing, defending, or trying to explain will only lead to escalation.

Learn the signs of when your partner-parent is crossing into irrationality so you can put up your emotional insulation, and teach your children to do the same. Having a signal that you can give the children to indicate when they should put up their protective shield will make that process quick and efficient without enraging the NP/BP. Exiting the situation until the NP/BP calms down will help protect you and the children.

Courage

It takes courage to face the NP/BP when he/she is being so loud, passionate, frantic, and extreme. The NP/BP is determined to be in control and to convince you that they're right. Talking and fighting back only increases their anger and fear. It's does nothing to pacify them or deescalate the situation.

Usually, the best reaction is to get away until he/she calms down. There is absolutely no way to bring the NP/BP back to reality by talking. You will need to develop the courage to exit the situation as soon as possible. Protecting yourself and the children has to be your priority. Walk away. Don't talk. Don't make a scene. Just take the children and leave the room or, if necessary, leave the house for a while. Go to a park, the grocery store, or visit a friend. Make it pleasant for the children. A narcissist/borderline person usually calms down within an hour or so when they have no one to attack.

When you return, be observant of their emotional state. They may be silent and exuding hostile energy. They may, however, act perfectly normal as if nothing happened. Have the courage to not discuss or engage the NP/BP until he/she is ready. Keep to your routines with the children. Don't mention the episode or try to talk things out. The NP/BP is unlikely to remember things accurately, and there's no need to rekindle those emotions again. Have the courage to leave things unsettled. But don't forget that these episodes will continue to happen cyclically and be prepared.

Building Your Strength

Make a Plan

Determination and courage can be called up best when you have a plan for your life and your parenting, Plans require goals and selected actions. It helps to have both big-picture life goals and everyday goals.

Whether you know it or not, you've probably had a goal of either waiting for the narcissist/borderline parent to see the light and get better, or of trying to change him/her using logic and explanations. Neither of these goals will ever reach fruition. There is nothing you can do to fix or change their emotional instability and delusions.

Think, instead, about the goals you want for yourself, your children, and your relationship. What you choose each day will either lead you toward or away from those goals. If you haven't done so, take time to write out specifically what you want to accomplish for yourself in life, what you want to provide for your children, and what you want in your relationship. Keep in mind that *your goals can only reflect what you, yourself, can accomplish.* You have no power to determine what your partner-parent chooses to do.

Then ask yourself: Are the actions and decisions I am currently making leading me to my goals? If not, then it's time to figure out the changes you need to make. When you have clear goals, it's much easier to see the choices you really want to make in the present, and not get side-tracked by the narcissist/borderline's emotional distractions.

Self-Encouragement

When both partners are emotionally healthy, they depend on each other for encouragement, direction, and validation. However, you can't rely on any of these things from a narcissistic/borderline partner. You will have to be your own encourager. It's essential to talk to yourself using positive reminders, reassurance, and loving encouragement. It will also be important to be around friends and other people who are rational, positive, encouraging, and uplifting.

Marie

When Marie came to therapy, she felt alone, unappreciated, and confused. Her husband had many signs of narcissistic/borderline behaviors.

She kept expecting him to help her, support her efforts, and be on her side, but she was continually disappointed and shocked by his self-centeredness and emotional outbursts. We discussed the reality of her situation, and she created new goals and expectations that would depend *only* on her own efforts. She hired reliable child care, went back to work, started her own savings account, made new friends, and started being more independent and self-caring. She learned to not engage in ineffectual arguments with her husband, and she took primary responsibility for caring for the children. At first, she expected this would all be too overwhelming, but she found that with the reliable support from others and the increased social connections, she actually felt less stressed and discouraged. In fact, she reported that she had more hope and an increasing sense of satisfaction with her life.

You know yourself better than anyone else does. You can be your own best supporter. Encourage yourself, and give yourself permission to do what feels right to you. Choose to say no when you don't want to do something. And take new steps to move toward your goals. These actions increase your courage and give you more hope and determination. When your children see you being more assertive and courageous, they'll be encouraged as well.

Self-Confidence
All of these new actions will increase your self-confidence. When you're depending on an emotionally unstable person to direct your life, it can be scary and hopeless. When you take over making your own decisions, base your actions on reality, and have a plan to care for yourself and your children, you'll feel much more grounded, stronger, and in control of your life.

Gather Your Resources

Information
If you're just realizing that your partner/parent may have narcissistic/borderline traits, do some research. There are lots of books and websites devoted to these disorders. Check the bibliography at the end of this book for reliable, scientifically based resources. No individual will have

all of the traits and behaviors listed. Usually if they have 60 to 70 percent of the traits once or twice a month or more frequently, you'll need
to seriously accept that they will continue to be impaired. Accepting
your situation as it really is will help you make decisions that benefit
and protect you and your children.

You'll also benefit from information about your own caretaker
tendencies. It's likely that you, too often, give in to things you don't
agree with, go along with crazy beliefs and behaviors, feel intimidated
by threats, harbor negative opinions about yourself, and too easily
discount or forget the narcissist/borderline's hostile behaviors. Learn
how you inadvertently reinforce the narcissist/borderline's negative
behaviors. Change your responses so that you and your children are
better protected. See the bibliography for resources that help you stop
caretaking the other adult in this relationship and help you focus more
on caring for your children.

Supporters
You'll need a circle of supporters to break away from the emotional
control of a narcissist/borderline partner. They'll need to be emotionally healthy people on whom you can rely for insight, encouragement,
corroboration, and even legal and financial help. Partnering with a
NP/BP has pulled you into a world of false beliefs, distorted reality, and
circular arguments that can confuse and distract you. It'll be important
to have people who can keep you grounded and on track and help you
appropriately care for your children. It's important not to fall into the
chaos but also not to become so hostile and paranoid that you over-
react.

Protections
Information, support people, goals, courage, and self-confidence all
help you protect your own sanity and build up your internal strengths
and sense of self. These are the building blocks of resilience. Knowing
the truth about yourself and your situation can help you prepare for the
chaos and protect you against the fallacious assertions of the NP/BP.
When you are emotionally well insulated and adequately supported,
you can better protect your children as well.

Finances

Whenever you are financially dependent on a narcissist/borderline person, you are subject to their control. They can use the threat of withholding money in order to coerce you to comply with their demands. They can also control what advantages your children have for sports, school, vacations, and other activities.

Narcissists are especially manipulative about money and often create all kinds of money schemes. Be careful about getting involved with their mythical beliefs and fantasies around money. You may need separate legal and financial advice to deal with this complicated issue.

Having control of some amount of money will help you support your children's needs and interests. Give serious consideration to how you can have a financial cushion for you and your children when the NP/BP overspends, loses on poor investments, or refuses to provide. When it comes to money, the NP/BP is rarely a cooperative partner.

Health

Health is essential to your helping your children be resilient, because when your mental or physical health becomes compromised, your children will lose their primary source of nurturing and emotional support. When you're overstressed, confused, fearful, or trying to appease the NP/BP, your physical as well as mental health can deteriorate. People in your relationship situation often become depressed, anxious, and are susceptible to migraines, poor eating habits, high blood pressure, and auto-immune disorders. Increasing your emotional strength and resilience can really help reduce your stress and anxiety and give you more hope and resolve.

Implementation

Always Have a Plan B

Throughout this book are ideas to help you create a plan to reinforce and increase your own and your children's resilience, self-confidence, success, and happiness. Every family is different, and as your children grow, your goals will grow with them. So, your plan will keep evolving. However, basing your goals on your values, standards, and ethical principles will keep you on target.

Because you'll always be, in some way, relating to a narcissistic/borderline partner/parent concerning your children, you will always need a Plan B. That is, you'll need to have a backup plan for any interaction or event in which the other parent participates. Plan B is your exit plan, or your "work around" plan for you and your children in case the NP/BP explodes, melts down, or becomes intolerable. Although many interactions may go well, never be complacent.

Persistence
Persistence is one of the essential skills you'll need to keep your resilience steady over time. NP/BPs are rigid, stubborn, and obstinate. Standing your ground with them means learning to repeat your choices and decisions over and over again. You'll need to continually identify and protect your emotional and physical boundaries and limits. Just when you think everything is normal or even getting better, the same old patterns will appear again. Learning to be even more persistent than the NP/BP can lead you to becoming stronger than you might have guessed.

Keep Going

Celebrate the Small Things
There is no perfect solution. In life you never "get there." It's a continuous process of learning and growing. Life changes day to day. Don't wait to be happy or satisfied until everything is just as you hoped. Celebrate all the small, daily accomplishments. Share the joys your children have each day. Be involved with them and cherish each success. Be there to support them in their losses, hurts, and insecurities. Listen, engage, and be part of their daily activities. Small conversations in the car on the way to soccer can mean a lot. Engage them in your activities with other families, cooking dinner, or doing a home project. It's really the small things that make the most difference in their lives and in yours.

It's a Long Run
Since your partner-parent will always have personality quirks and problems, you'll always have to be aware and prepared. Even if you split up, you will continue to be connected to some degree through your

children. Remember, too, when your children become adults, you'll be dealing with holidays, graduations, weddings, births, and deaths during which there are likely to be stresses, emotional triggers, and social difficulties due to the presence of the NP/BP. When your children become adults and get to choose whether and how to include their two parents, what do you hope will be the solution? Now is the time to build for that future. This is a long run process.

Give Yourself Credit

You'll be better able to sustain your strength, determination, and hope when you remember to give yourself credit for all you do. You didn't know you were taking on such a big job when you chose this partner-parent. Now you're here, and you want the best for your children and you're stepping up to do the best you can for them. Some days congratulating yourself for getting through one more day may be the best there is. But look around you, really see your children, feel your joy in them, consider all you do for them, and give yourself credit and recognition for what you're doing every minute of every day. You are changing their world. And it will be well worth it in the long run.

Gratitude

You may find it hard to feel gratitude at this time. But evidence supports the fact that when you tune in each day to what you're grateful for, you'll feel more hopeful about the future, more energy and satisfaction, and less stress. You have intelligence, health, support from others, beautiful children, resources, determination, and courage. The more you're thankful for what you have, the more resilience you'll have. It works.

Generosity

Although we have talked quite a bit about the difficulties and pain that the NP/BP has brought into your life, your partner-parent is someone you love or have loved. Try to have compassion for him/her. NPD and BPD are cyclical forms of mental illness. Symptoms appear and disappear suddenly and without provocation. Your partner doesn't enjoy being so angry and out of control. He/she didn't choose to have this illness. When you compare your emotional life to theirs, your ability for empathy and emotional connection, your level of happiness and theirs—which would you choose?

Practice being positive, accepting, and generous when she/he is doing well emotionally, while also being prepared to deal with sudden changes in mood and demeanor. Encourage your children to enjoy the other parent's positive traits and activities, and also help them learn to protect themselves from emotional harm. Assuredly, this back and forth is challenging, but it's what you have. We're hoping this book will help make your family interactions more successful and healthy.

CHAPTER EIGHT

~

Self-Compassion
Key to Developing Healthy Self-Worth

As a parent, you probably see one of your most important roles is to raise confident, happy children who feel good about themselves, make positive choices, and are well prepared to become healthy, contributing adults. When you're in a family with a NP/BP partner-parent, helping your children develop self-worth is both critically important and challenging.

For many years, psychologists and child development experts believed that building self- esteem in children was the best means of developing a healthy sense of self-worth. However, more current research suggests that self-compassion is a much more effective building block to self-worth. So, what's the difference?

Self-Esteem

At its most basic, self-esteem is made up of the opinions we hold about ourselves—how we feel about our personal value and our worth. Self-esteem is based on social *comparison*. In order to be chosen for an honor, win the competition, receive the trophy, and more, a child must be better than the others. This type of social comparison is often accompanied by feeling superior to everyone else, or putting others down in order to feel better, rise to the top, or win. One particularly damaging aspect of having to be better than everyone else in order to have good self-esteem is that it creates the belief that being average is undesirable. Yet for the great majority of us, our lives consist of mostly ordinary, average moments.

This makes self-worth dependent solely on being better than everyone else. It also makes a person more vulnerable to anxiety, depression, and even insecurity when things don't go as planned. This roller coaster of self-esteem earned by being the best when you win and feeling like a failure when you don't is exhausting, and frankly unrealistic. It may help to think of self-esteem as a balloon that when inflated appears strong and beautiful. But balloons are also quite fragile and easily popped. When that happens, there is nothing left inside but emptiness.

This up and down self-esteem is one of the core elements of people with narcissistic or borderline characteristics. Internally narcissists feel like a failure—unloveable and afraid others will find out that their façade of being perfect and always right is a fake, while people with borderline features rarely feel like they're acceptable or can measure up. Both focus their entire sense of self-worth on what other people think. As parents, they tend to compare their children to others and demand unrealistic standards of perfection. So, they continually feel disappointed in their children. This can lead to discouraged children with low motivation and a poor sense of their own abilities. Instead, we highly recommend that you help your children find their sense of self-worth through self-compassion instead of comparison to arbitrary standards.

Self-Compassion

Compassion researcher Kristen Neff, PhD[1] suggests that self-compassion provides the same benefits as high self-esteem but without the toxic drawbacks of constant comparison to others, or earned through being special and above average and solely contingent upon success. Dr. Neff defines self-compassion as having three core components: *self-kindness*, where we are gentle and understanding with ourselves instead of being critical and judgmental; recognition of our *common humanity*, where we understand that as human beings we are in this life together rather than being alone and isolated; and *mindfulness*, where we are aware of our experiences in the present moment. True self-compassion is the combination of all three of these components.

In more than a decade of research, Dr. Neff and her colleagues have repeatedly found that "self-compassion is the perfect alternative to the relentless pursuit of self-esteem."[2] The benefits of self-compassion are significant.

- reduced anxiety and depression
- less shame and/or embarrassment when things don't go well
- steadier, more consistent sense of self-worth that carries into adulthood
- stronger overall coping skills
- greater well-being
- compassion for others

If we use the analogy of self-esteem as a balloon, perhaps we can envision self-compassion as something more solid, like an apple. It's the substance within that gives the apple its shape on the outside. Even when something happens to the outside, the inside remains solid.

In chapter 15 we will describe specific ways to help your children develop their own self-compassion. An additional benefit of helping your children build self-compassion is that you'll increase your own self-compassion as well.

Why Self-Compassion Is Critical for Children

When a parent has narcissistic/borderline traits, the focus of the family tends to always be on them. There is no room for anyone else to have a separate opinion, a challenging thought, or be different from that parent in any way. Normally, parents serve as mirrors for their children, reflecting their personality qualities back to them, helping them gain confidence, develop, and grow. In families where a parent is narcissistic or borderline, the parent-child role is reversed. Instead of the parent reflecting the child's wants, needs, interests, and experiences, the children are expected to be the mirror that reflects the NP/BP's views, feelings, and needs. In addition, too often *your* attention is continually pulled away from the children to handle the dramas and needs of your partner-parent. The time and opportunities for children to develop a healthy sense of self then take a backseat, or can even be nonexistent. Children of narcissists and borderlines often feel:

- invisible
- never good enough
- deeply afraid to express thoughts or feelings
- chronically unsure of themselves
- deeply insecure
- overly sensitive
- unable to trust others, especially adults

How to Help

As the caretaking parent in a NP/BP family, you face a big task. You must do almost all of the emotional parenting, and in some cases, the physical, day-to-day parenting as well. You also have to intervene when you see your children being emotionally, or even physically, attacked by the narcissistic/borderline parent. There are many actions you can take to support your child's developing self-compassion, which can counterbalance the negative effects from the other parent. Your calm, steady presence and day-to-day support are tremendously important in providing a healthy, safe, secure environment for your children.

Keep Your Children Safe

You are their safe port in the storm. In a home that often feels chaotic, stressful, and unpredictable, you must be able to stay strong and focused enough to keep your children's safety at the forefront of your choices. You must know when to give your children a "time out" from the other parent, or when to remove them altogether. It is this safe emotional container that you place around your children that will provide an opportunity for them to develop a sense of worth and self-confidence.

Teach Self-Calming Techniques

Learning to soothe ourselves when we feel stressed or anxious is a valuable, lifelong skill. Many self-calming techniques are incredibly simple.

For example, take a few deep breaths, or hold your hand over your heart as you inhale and exhale. This initiates a cascade of calming in your central nervous system. Another way to self-soothe is to get physical. Encourage your child to do some simple stretches, squeeze a ball, ride a bike or scooter, or simply go outside to play. You can also change the scenery. Watch a funny movie, play with a pet, read a favorite book, or take a rest.

Also, help your children learn to tune in to their bodies and learn to identify what they need. Teach them it's OK to ask for what they need. For example, get a drink of water, or if hungry, have a snack, ask for cuddle time with a safe adult, or spend quiet time alone.

Each time you and your children initiate a calming action in a stressful situation, you'll gain confidence and feel more empowered, which reduces the stress you're experiencing. These techniques will work wonders for your children and your own well-being too.

Help Your Children Learn and Practice Self-Compassion

Self-esteem must be tempered with self-compassion so that it doesn't morph into a competition of always having to be best, first, and never wrong. Narcissistic/borderline parents too often bring very little kindness to their children. Instead they parent with criticism, shame, and judgment, all of which are terribly toxic to a child's fragile sense of self. Self-compassion is a way to counter this toxicity.

Self-compassion means treating your own thoughts, actions, and needs with gentleness and caring consideration, instead of criticism and reproach. Instituting compassionate parenting into your home will help to neutralize the more harsh, demanding child-rearing methods of the narcissistic/borderline parent. In chapter 15 we'll discuss specific ways for you to help your children develop more self-compassion.

Teach Problem-Solving Techniques

You're a great resource for your children when it comes to helping them solve personal problems. Your task isn't to actually solve the problem, but to act as an advisor or coach to help your children work out their own solutions. The process of identifying the problem, generating possible solutions, taking action, and then talking about how well it worked strengthens their self-confidence.

As you know, figuring out the core issues of a problem can be very difficult in a household with a narcissistic/borderline parent. Their confusion about reality, delusional beliefs, and poor communication skills can make problem solving very difficult. We'll cover specific steps of problem solving for your complicated family in chapter 13.

Model Effective Communication Skills

Good communication is a skill that can be learned. There are two ways for you to help your children develop their own effective communication skills. *First*, in your day-to-day interactions with your children and others, model good communication. Listen, be present, ask clarifying questions if needed, be open to alternative points of view, and remain calm and keep your anger under control.

And *second*, find opportunities for mini talks with your children about the communication skills you are using. Here's an example: You are all at the grocery store picking up some ice cream for a birthday party, and you're hurrying because you're afraid you'll be late. In the checkout line, another customer with a very full cart of groceries rudely cuts in front of you. Here's how the mini talk could go: "Remember that time in the grocery store when we were hurrying to Lisa's birthday party and the woman cut in line in front of us? Well, I was pretty frustrated, and my first reaction was to get mad at her. But you know what I did? I took a big breath, and then another one. I looked around and saw that all the lines were full so it wasn't worth trying to move. And she had that fussy baby in the seat. I bet she just wanted to get that baby home. I told myself that we still had enough time. Those deep breaths helped me calm down and realize that I could choose not to be upset. And, we still got to the party in time."

These conversations give your children valuable lessons about how to handle real-life situations more effectively. And because you're talking about how *you* handled something, it's less threatening than if you were talking about something *they* did. Also, sharing examples of how you've learned to calmly and effectively talk with the narcissistic/borderline parent will provide an explicit model without criticism. This will make it a more comfortable teaching moment, and easier for your child to incorporate the learning.

Be Available to Listen

When your child is talking to you, give your full attention. This is the time to set your phone or other devices aside. Face-to-face interactions signal that you are fully present and attending to what your child is saying. It gives your children the message that what they have to say is important to you. Narcissistic/borderline parents tend to take up most of the conversation airtime in the family, so it is crucial that your children have their own opportunities to talk and really be heard, have their feelings validated, and their needs responded to. It can take a few extra minutes, but it can provide wonderful support for your children's healthy self-esteem.

Set Clear Boundaries

When children know the rules and what is expected of them, they have much greater opportunities to be successful. Setting clear boundaries provides emotional safety for children and will help them develop self-trust as well as trust in others. Positive predictability over time provides a sense of security. And when you demonstrate ways to set and defend clear boundaries with the narcissistic/borderline parent, you'll provide a healthy model for your children.

Validate Your Children's Feelings—All of Them

There is no such thing as a wrong feeling, although narcissistic/borderline parents will often discount or deny any feelings other than their own. It is crucial that you provide a counterbalance by recognizing and honoring your child's feelings. Give words to help your children understand their feelings. For example, "When I brought your lunch to your classroom, you seemed embarrassed." Or, "It sounds like you were disappointed when Dad didn't come to your soccer match." When you identify and name their feelings, it helps your children learn to use words instead of acting out their feelings. This gives them a sense of self-control and the ability to communicate more effectively.

Give Positive, Realistic Feedback

The narcissistic/borderline parent's reality is often skewed. It makes it hard for your children to develop their own identity or know what they really feel or want, because everything is about what the parent wants. NP/BPs see their children primarily as reflections of themselves, with no separate individuality of their own. When you offer realistic, positive feedback, you give your children a more authentic view of themselves.

When giving feedback, it's important to discuss the *action* rather than the *person*. For example, instead of saying, "You are a good boy for cleaning your room," you might say something like this: "You worked so hard cleaning your room. Look how you lined up your cars on the shelves. I bet it feels good to be able to see all of them."

In this way your children learn that the hard work to clean their room pays off for themselves as well as for positive recognition. This helps them have a sense of accomplishment and perhaps even pride in a job well done. And it helps them internalize the belief that they are good workers and can contribute and be helpful, which strengthens their sense of self-confidence. It is the accumulation of multiple opportunities for this kind of helpful, realistic feedback that develops healthy self-esteem.

Don't Overpraise but Give Acknowledgment

Give reasonable, realistic encouragement and support. Overpraising doesn't help, and in fact it does more harm than good to self-esteem. Competence doesn't grow from praise, but it comes from taking age-appropriate risks, being responsible for their actions, trying, failing, making choices, and solving problems. Children need to feel that they are capable of contributing, facing difficulties, and learning new skills.[3] Commenting on their accomplishments and good feelings about themselves helps them acknowledge their success. For example:

- I appreciated your help today in making dinner.
- I'll bet it felt good to get your science project finished.
- I know it has been hard for you to practice your flute every day, but you looked so proud of yourself at the recital last night.
- Thank you for washing the car for me. It feels so good to be driving around in a clean car.

Create Ways for Children to Feel Successful

Help your children pursue interests outside of the home where they can be challenged and find their own success. With their input, get them involved in extracurricular activities such as sports, drama, scouting, 4-H, and the like. As children master the ins and outs of an activity and have opportunities to learn to interact with their peers, their sense of mastery grows. They learn the value of teamwork, face challenges, and develop resilience—especially when they lose a game or don't get chosen for the role they hoped for. These are powerful and important life lessons. Extracurricular activities also provide access to other adults who can serve as positive role models.

Watch for Emotional Problems and Dysregulation

Notice if your child shows extreme emotional reactions to situations, has trouble regulating responses to provocative stimuli, has frequent anger outbursts, or has trouble calming down. Extremely rigid thinking and behaviors, feelings that are very easily and strongly triggered, and inability to take other people's feelings into consideration can be signs that your child needs professional support and assistance.

These behaviors signal that it's time to find a therapist who is familiar with the complicated emotional system of families with a narcissistic/borderline parent. A good therapist can provide a safe, friendly environment where your child can begin to explore the family dynamics and learn to understand and handle the emotions that feel so out of control.

All parents want their children to grow up with a healthy sense of who they are and feel competent and confident about their abilities. Gaining self-worth is a normal developmental process of childhood; however, not all families are able to provide the authentic feedback and nurturing that leads to healthy self-worth. Having a narcissistic/borderline partner-parent means that you'll have additional challenges that that must addressed to help your children develop into emotionally strong and resilient beings. Teaching your children self-compassion and modeling it in your interactions with them and with others will go a long way toward giving them a kind of life skills multivitamin. It will fill in the nurturing, attention, reality-based information, understanding, and acceptance that may be chronically in short supply from the narcissistic/borderline parent. In chapter 11 we'll dig into strategies you can use to help your children develop and increase their self-compassion.

~

CHAPTER NINE

Creating an Environment to Thrive

In order to be the responsive and resilient parent that we're describing, you'll need to create an environment where you and your children can thrive. This needs to be more calm, positive, accepting, and mindful than is typical in families with a narcissistic or borderline parent. Although you won't be able to directly change how your partner-parent talks and behaves, you can create a subenvironment based on your attachment and parenting relationship with your children.

This chapter covers the elements of how to build a resilient, consistent environment where your children can be guaranteed that you will listen, consider, and respond to their feelings, needs, and individuality. You don't have to fall into the narcissistic family system described earlier. You can create a dependable, loving relationship with your children using positive, time-tested parenting behaviors despite whatever ups and downs your partner-parent may going through.[1]

Secure, Primary Attachment

This begins with a secure, abiding, and durable connection to your children in which you are more loyal and primary to them than to your partner-parent. We know that this is quite different than the advice you hear from most counselors and the culture in general that it's more important to make your partner relationship primary. However, the relationship with your narcissist/borderline partner will never be reliable, rational, consistently healthy, or in anyone's best interest except their own. It cannot be the basis for trustworthy parenting. Therefore, you'll need to create a parenting model that relies just on you and other supportive family and friends for the dependability needed. At the same time, we do suggest and encourage respect and positive interactions between yourself, the children, and your partner-parent whenever possible.

Your goal is to give your children a sense of stability, trust, reliability, openness, warmth, and acceptance. This will help create greater stability for your children to grow and learn healthy self-compassion and positive relationship behaviors. Because of the NP/BP's inability to be consistently loving and able to see the child as a separate person, their attachment relationship with their children tends to be what is called "ambivalent or insecure."[2] They fluctuate from love to hostility, to outright rejection, to suffocation, and back again, which is very hard to trust. As a result, your children will tend to shift between trying to please the NP/BP parent to being afraid of him/her.

Making your parent-child relationship primary means giving much greater energy and importance to the children's needs over the needs of the NP/BP. It does not, however, mean babying, pampering, or conversely elevating your children into adult status. You need to maintain your role as parent to your children, not confidant or co-conspirator. To do this you'll have to increase your emotional power in the family, which your partner-parent will likely resist if it is too overt or hostile. However, there are many subtle ways to make this happen.

Consistent Routines

One basic thing that can set the tone for less chaos and more calm are consistent routines. Everyone in the family will benefit from predictable mealtimes, bedtimes, and chores. Routines help keep a steady rhythm to the day. They can also provide specific times for you and your children to spend time together; for example, making meals together, cleaning up, listening about their day, reading stories at bedtime, doing homework, exercising, and playing games.

Rituals can also tie the family together. Recurring events like birthdays, holidays, and celebrating achievements give children something special to look forward to. Baking cookies, hanging ornaments on the tree, special foods, and spending time together outside the busy work schedule offer opportunities to pass down family stories and puts emphasis on your connection with your children.

Boundaries

We suggest taking over as much of the parenting responsibilities as possible, such as getting children ready for school, supervising homework, overseeing children's chores, bedtime rituals, taking children to school, and arranging care after school. Homeschooling children is highly discouraged. It is often used by the NP/BP to isolate the family from normal and natural community connections and thus create more isolation and control over the family members.

Refuse to participate in arguments with the NP/BP. Defuse, redirect, and, if necessary, remove yourself and the children from hostile, argumentative situations. Continuing to "discuss" issues with an antagonistic person is counterproductive and will typically escalate the situation.

Do not get caught up in name-calling, yelling, door banging, or other temper-tantrum behaviors. Do everything possible to stay calm, and keep the best interests of the children in mind. Be respectful, but also be firm in your behaviors and decisions. You want to choose your actions, not just blindly respond out of anger and frustration.

Logical, Minimal Rules

There are two logical, minimal rules that cover a lot of situations: don't do anything to harm yourself, and don't purposely harm anyone else. All other guidelines flow from these two principles. Even quite young children can see when an action hurts themselves or hurts others. Talk with your children about the behaviors that help family members get along with each other. Ask them to identify their own feelings and to interpret the feelings of others around them, so they can learn to be self-aware and understanding of others.

These are lessons that the NP/BP will not likely be skilled in doing. When children pay attention to their own feelings and needs as well as tuning into what others are experiencing, they learn empathy, cooperation, and teamwork. The focus is then on working together rather than obeying or resisting rules.

Modeling

The very best way to teach your children how to behave is to model the behavior you want them to use. Young children tune in mostly to body language, while older children enjoy exploring words. Notice the messages you say to yourself and out loud. Your children will copy what you say and do. How you interact with them and with your partner-parent will be significant in their learning about relationships.

If you want your children to say please and thank you, use those words a lot with them. Thank them for the things they do like picking up toys, speaking kindly, sharing, or even giving you a hug. Ask them politely to help you with tasks that fit their abilities. Include them in everything you do around the home, such as shopping, visiting, talking with people at school, and more. Show them how to behave. You may even find it helpful to talk with them about events you have shared together and ask them what they enjoyed, what they noticed, and what they think about how things happened. Showing interest and caring about others is a wonderful skill to pass on to your children.

Mirroring

Acknowledging what you notice about your children helps them feel seen and heard. This is called mirroring. Notice, identify and validate the positive behaviors you see, such as caring, helping, and sharing. Calmly comment on behavior mistakes without criticism; for example, "I think that hurt Sarah's feelings. What do you think?" or "When you took Jeffery's toy, he started to cry. What do you think he was feeling?" Identify and name the feelings you see in your children. "You seem very annoyed today with your brother," or "You're looking quite pleased with this picture you drew."

Children who are seen and heard develop greater self-confidence. They feel a sense of acceptance and belonging, and they feel stronger and more sure of themselves in the world. In other words, they thrive.

Culture of Kindness

What we're describing here is creating what Kristen Neff calls a "Culture of Kindness."[3] Instead of going along with the destructive patterns of the NFS, we're suggesting that you create a thriving environment of kindness, encouragement, and connection. The NP/BP may or may not choose to join in. You, however, will set the tone for how you want to interact and parent your children. Here are some ways to deal with these two distinct types of parenting.

Safety

Creating a sense of safety is important for your children to feel comfortable to be themselves. Neff identifies three ways to create safety in difficult circumstances: close down, leave, and take action. Any of these three may be appropriate and effective in different circumstances. In chapter 11, we'll talk about effective techniques to respond when a narcissistic/borderline parent is acting out and creating a scary situation.

It's important to keep in mind that it will be your job to choose the appropriate reactions when chaos and anger erupt from the narcissist/borderline parent. Even if you're not present when an alarming and inappropriate situation happens, you can do a lot to help your children understand and cope. You can help your children talk through their feelings, reassure them, and help them understand the NP/BP's anger and blame wasn't caused by them, but by the feelings inside the NP/BP, and it is not their fault.

Your close, positive connection with your children will provide the emotional safety net they need. Your courage, strength, and caring will help them recover and make sense of their experiences. Focusing on their needs for safety, instead of your fears, can help you assess the situation, take clear-headed actions, and assist them in managing their feelings.

Accepting Imperfection

Nobody is perfect. However, in the NFS perfection is often demanded. Your ability to accept imperfection in yourself, your children, and your partner-parent will be essential for creating a kinder family environment. Learning to navigate and manage interactions while keeping the weaknesses and vulnerabilities of each person in mind can make a huge difference in how your family functions.

Every person has unique difficulties, fears, and issues that may or may not be adjustable. Acknowledging these problems enables you to anticipate reactions and have a plan to respond effectively. Life isn't about fixing everyone until they are just the way you want them to be. Life is about learning to function despite the shortcomings and imperfections in ourselves and others.

Surprisingly, research shows that acceptance leads to a greater likelihood of change than criticism, demands, and punishment. When we're criticized, we tend to close down and become stubborn. Whereas, when we can acknowledge a problem, it seems easier to look at it as something to be solved rather than defended. Acceptance also allows you to anticipate more accurately what is likely to happen and have a plan to deal with it.

Honesty

To be an effective parent in this unusual family, you'll need to face your situation honestly. You need to never lose sight of the facts of your family's circumstances or be lulled into thinking that everything will magically get better someday. Some days and months will be better, but personality disorders never go away. Accepting the facts and staying aware will be immensely helpful in being a truly helpful, caring parent. It is the basis of protecting and nurturing your children through their developmental years.

Honestly tune into your true feelings and wants for your own life. Hiding your true feelings, especially from yourself, leads to poor choices, disappointment, and a life heading in the wrong direction. The relationship with your partner isn't what you expected, but now you have children together, and you have an important job to do now and for the rest of their lives. But you also have your own life to live.

Given the circumstances you're in, what do you see are the best options for you as well as your children? When you look at your life clearly and honestly and make your choice about what you want to do, make a commitment to embrace that choice fully. When you have a clear path for your life, then you'll be a strong and healthy role model for your children. Your courage gives your children courage and a greater trust that you can keep them safe.

Tools You Will Need

Inner Strength, Outer Support

Whatever path you choose will take determination and emotional strength. You'll need to identify your parenting and personal values and devise a life plan that truly embodies these values. Knowing what's important to you gives you strength and resolve to face your fears and take the actions necessary to make a life where you and your children can thrive.

You'll need to keep your goals constantly in mind. Parenting will take more of your attention than usual. It can't be an after-thought, and you can't accomplish it without a plan. However, it's not going to take up every minute of your life. Building a positive work life and social community will greatly enhance your ability to cope with the difficulties at home.

You'll need a strong support system of healthy family members, friends, teachers, a therapist for you and probably for the children. You'll need a sense of emotional independence. And you'll need to build financial independence as well. When you have strong values, a worthwhile goal, and support from others, you'll have the strength you need to be successful.

Resilient Coping

You're going to need your own resilience to face these difficult situations—not of your choosing. Your partner-parent has a disability that makes him or her less able to be an effective parent or be a loving spouse than you expected. In addition, he/she is blind to the facts of their own inability and shortcomings. This puts a big responsibility on you to figure out how to cope on your own. As outlined in chapter 5, we suggest that you use the five components of resilience identified by Linda Graham[4] to cope more effectively in your situation.

Calming yourself and your children. Difficult situations can be greatly improved by creating and maintaining a sense of inner calm. Practicing calming breathing, calming thinking, and even counting to ten can be very helpful. These help the body disengage the primitive fight, flight, or freeze responses that impede rational thinking in a highly charged situation. Staying calm when your partner-parent is emotionally distraught can help you stay out of useless conflicts and help your children be less frightened.

Clarity keeps your mind calm, your options and choices clear, and helps you stay grounded in reality instead of fear, hope, guilt, or confusion. When you can stay clear on the facts as well as your goals, values, and choices, you can continue to provide security and stability for yourself and your children.

Connection to people, to sanity, and to the real world outside the rigid walls of the narcissist/borderline's delusional mind is essential to your well-being. When you are isolated and encased in the chaotic misperceptions on your partner-parent, you can quickly lose your own reasoning powers. You definitely need to stay connected to a healthy support system and rational thinking.

Competence in understanding the emotional disabilities of your partner-parent, as well as the needs of your children's mental and emotional development, will be necessary. Read, talk to professionals, reach out for help. The more you know, the more you'll be prepared to calmly respond to each chaotic experience as it appears. Learn the skills suggested by professionals, practice being more assertive and taking charge, and take good care of your physical and emotional health.

Courage makes all the difference in the long run. You have to marshal your courage to take actions that your volatile partner-parent may not like. Even if you've felt afraid to stand up for yourself, you'll probably find that it's easier to gather your courage to protect your children from harm. They certainly need your help, and they are relying on you to make sense of what they're feeling and experiencing.

Let Go of Guilt

You won't be able to create a loving, kind, thriving connection with your children as long as you are caught in the throes of guilt. We have never talked with a parent with a NP/BP partner-parent who didn't have strong feelings of guilt—guilt for picking this partner, guilt for ever having children, guilt for how the partner behaves, guilt for staying, guilt for leaving, guilt for so much.

Guilt drains your energy, saps your determination, and questions your every move. Guilt keeps you stuck doing nothing. The NP/BP constantly tries to trigger your guilt, because she/he intuitively knows that it keeps you from taking new action. Your partner wants to be in control and have everything his/her way. When you have no energy, feel hopeless, and even helpless, your partner has the power to make him/herself feel secure while making everyone else miserable.

You are not responsible for the behaviors of your partner-parent. You need to do what you can to protect your children, but even with your best efforts, they will be affected by the emotional turmoil of the NP/BP—just as you have been. You can't eliminate those effects entirely.

Don't Demonize the Narcissistic/Borderline Parent

Remember, too, that the other parent also brings many positive and important experiences into your children's lives as well. Children are very aware of having qualities and traits from each parent. They want to feel proud of the positive qualities they get from each parent. When you constantly act distraught, angry, and miserable about the other parent, children personalize that to mean they, too, are damaged or bad. Help them identify qualities in the NP/BP parent that are positive, while at the same time choosing more positive behaviors and reactions yourself.

Remember, your children have an entirely different relationship with the other parent than you have. They don't react in the same ways that you do because they have had different experiences with this parent. Don't assume that what they experience is all bad. Don't assume that they can't handle themselves alone with the other parent. We've seen children handle their disabled parent's quirks and misbehaviors sometimes better than the other parent. Give your kids credit for being aware, competent, and able to handle what life brings. You can be there to help if they stumble, but you're not responsible for everything that happens to them.

Letting go of your guilt, facing the facts, thinking through your options, making good choices, and having the courage to follow through will create the environment for your children and yourself to have a better life.

CHAPTER TEN

~

Responsive Parenting

At the heart of this book, and we believe, in your heart as a parent, is your abiding love and concern for your children and how to give them the best and most effective parenting you are able to provide, in the family situation in which you live. Fortunately, we've never met a parent who starts his or her day by saying, "Today I'm going to ruin my child." Indeed, there are times when through a parent's actions or life experiences, children's lives are damaged, sometimes quite significantly. But it is extremely rare that a parent deliberately sets out to damage a child. There is usually a long list of contributing factors, some within a parent's control and some not at all in their control that may yield devastating results for their children. The task then becomes to counteract those factors that can obstruct the kind of parenting your children need. And that takes knowledge, practice, and a lot of support.

You are already ahead because you are seeking information and help to improve your parenting skills. I (Jean) have a colleague that teaches parenting classes. He begins each new session by stating how helpful it would be if children came with a booklet of operating instructions, like we might receive with a new dishwasher or vehicle. He goes on to lament that no such instructions come attached to the tiny toes of our newborns. In many respects, parents are on their own to figure out what works and what doesn't work. Parenting is very much on-the-job training, or as one discouraged parent of a toddler commented to me, her parenting style felt like the title of the old Clint Eastwood movie, *The Good, the Bad and the Ugly.*

At one time or another, every new parent, along with some very experienced ones, will be baffled as to how to effectively handle a particular situation with their children. At each stage of your child's development, your bewilderment will likely continue to challenge and frustrate you. This is simply a normal part of parenting. There is an abundance of excellent parenting books available to help you learn about your children's needs and how to support them to grow and thrive.

In a narcissistic family system, the parenting challenges and frustrations are not only greater than in families without a narcissistic/borderline parent, they are also different. As the non-NP/BP parent, you have a big job—a huge job really. It falls to you to respond in ways that counteract the emotional destruction that usually comes from having a narcissistic parent, and day by day, interaction by interaction, help your children grow into confident, self-compassionate, resilient human beings. In the remainder of this chapter, we'll walk you through a variety of actions you can take to maximize your responsiveness as a parent and help your children.

Approach Your Parenting Mindfully

Start from Your Values

An important foundation in parenting is getting clear about your values. What's important to you as your raise your children? Are there broader family culture issues to consider? Another way to think about this is, what's your endgame in terms of your children? To the best of your ability, how do you want them to turn out? Parenting is never a straight line. It's much more like a bumpy, winding road, filled with potholes and many detours, but knowing your values is like having a really good map as a resource.

Once you are clear about the values that are important, you can then set household rules and boundaries that support those values. For example, if treating people with kindness is a value, then when siblings get into an argument and are calling each other names, you might intervene and say something like, "In this family we treat each other with respect and kindness. That means no name-calling. Find a way to solve the problem you have with each other without being unkind. I'm happy to help if you'd like." This might sound hypocritical since the NP/BP parent might often resort to unkind behaviors. It gives you many opportunities to help your children talk about how it feels when someone is unkind, and how they can be more resilient when it happens. Knowing what you value helps keep you going in the direction you want.

Establish a Secure Attachment

Healthy emotional development starts with a child being securely attached to his or her caregivers. While it may seem ideal for a child to be attached to both parents, research repeatedly shows that a secure attachment to *one parent* is enough to create a strong foundation for healthy development. Secure attachment starts in infancy when a child learns that a loving and trustworthy adult will consistently and predictably be available and responsive to meet her physical and emotional needs. By age two, a child's daily interactions with caregivers will determine her attachment style. Recent research in neuroscience tells us that having a secure parent-child bond is a vital safety cue for a child's developing nervous system, signaling that her environment is safe enough for her to venture into it, to explore and grow. These are critical milestones for healthy development. Dr. Sue Johnson[1] has coined the acronym *ARE* to include the components of secure attachment: Accessible, Responsive, and Engaged. In other words, *"Are you there for me?"* Secure attachment doesn't end with infancy but continues through life as your children grow through each of the stages of development. It also follows into adulthood and plays a key role in healthy relationships there as well.

Children have an inborn need to connect with those around them, and feel truly seen. When parents, teachers, and caregivers meet these needs for connection and validation, children develop secure attachment and a sense of emotional safety. They come to know that their immediate world is a safe place and their needs are important and will be met. This ongoing cycle of having an emotional need for connection, recognition, or validation, and then actually experiencing loving adults who meet those needs, builds a strong foundation for healthy social and emotional development.

Create a Safe Environment for Emotions

One of the most important things you can do for your children within your home is to create a safe environment for them to feel and express emotions. In gentle and encouraging actions, as you listen and talk with them, you can help your children explore their emotions and give names to what they are feeling. Emotions are neither good nor bad. They are reflections of how someone is feeling at any given moment in time. Emotions are also fluid—sometimes changing moment to moment. With your unconditional love and supportive presence, you help your children develop a working vocabulary for emotions, and learn that all emotions are acceptable. In an NFS, the NP/BP is likely to engage in actions that are the opposite of listening, such as discounting feelings, judging, and criticizing, rather than creating a safe container for all emotions. It then becomes your responsibility to protect your children's developing psyches.

Let's look at an example of how this safe emotional environment might work. You arrive home from the grocery store and walk into a screaming match between your husband and twelve-year-old son. Your husband is holding a grade report in his hand and shouting about how disappointed he is in your son because of the C he got in history. "How do you think this makes me look?" Your husband, a history professor, screams. "Can't you ever do anything right? Do you have any idea how embarrassing it is to have such a stupid kid?" Your son shakes his head and shrugs, then takes a seat in front of his gaming console and begins frantically shooting at targets on the screen. With each hit he shouts a loud, "Yes!" His actions are robotlike, except for the escalating shouts. You take a seat beside him, at first offering nothing but your presence. You're tempted to look at your watch knowing that you need to start dinner, but you don't. You are also tempted to snap at him to stop playing the game, which you don't like, and demand that he talk to you. But you know he's hurting from the things his dad said. You could leave him to distract himself from his feelings with the video game, but that wouldn't help him in the long run. So, you take a deep breath and dive in. "Dad said some pretty hurtful things to you just now," you begin. Your son may or may not respond to this first overture. Keep going. "If that had been me, I think I'd be feeling discouraged, because I know I worked hard for that grade. And maybe I'd be angry. Yeah, I think

I'd definitely feel angry." Then you wait. You've planted the seed and named some possible feelings your son may have. You don't try to distract him from his feelings. Nor do you try to talk him out of what he's experiencing. You wait. He may respond to what you've just said, or he may not. His response isn't nearly as important as your supportive presence. By sitting with him and acknowledging his pain, you've shown that you are there for him, that he matters, and that you understand. These are so very important for his sense of emotional safety, trust in you, and his overall awareness that his feelings do matter. You have opened the door to future discussions, questions, and opportunities for emotional connection and support.

Be Emotionally Present

Simply put, emotional presence consists of you giving your full attention to what is happening in the present moment. It is the opposite of being distracted or trying to multitask. Here are some basics that will help you be emotionally present with your children.

Make Eye Contact

Connecting face to face, eyeball to eyeball is a sure way to let your child know you are tuned in and paying attention. There are times when direct eye contact may feel too intense for your child. If that's the case, you might alternate looking away with direct eye contact. Sometimes you might be side by side and talking; for example, in the car or working together on a task like putting toys away or setting the table for a meal. In these instances, you have what I think of as "imaginary eye contact" where your focus and presence replace actual eye contact.

Watch Your Body Language

As best you can, present an open posture. Relax your body. No crossed arms, jiggling feet, or furtive glances at the television or phone. Smile or at least maintain a neutral expression that communicates your interest.

Put Down All Screens

No cell phones, computers, televisions, or games to distract either of you. Nothing is more frustrating than to be in the middle of an important discussion and have the person you are talking to look away, check their phone, answer a message, or stare at the television. These distractions convey that anyone or anything else is more important.

Come Close
Sit or stand close to your child. Try to arrange yourself at the same eye level as your child. Offer an encouraging touch on the arm or back. For the time you are talking with your child, let it be the ONLY thing you do.

Respond
As your child is telling you something, nod your head, smile, and make supportive sounds like "oh," "un-huh," and "mmm." You can also add, "I see," "Tell me more," "What else happened?" These are "listening sounds" that demonstrate that you are paying attention and show that you're interested.

Validate
Psychologist Rick Hanson, PhD[2] suggests five forms of caring that provide opportunities to validate children. They are: being included, seen, appreciated, liked, and loved. In your daily interactions, when you use these caring forms, your child feels truly seen and validated. It is the repetition of these caring behaviors over time that reinforces secure attachment and builds the framework of emotional health.

In your family there will be times when it is important for you to hear about an experience your child had with the NP/BP parent, and honor her truth. For example, "You're right, Dad yelled at you for no reason. You did nothing to deserve his anger. It wasn't fair." With this set of statements, you've given your daughter validation for her feelings, words to identify how she might be feeling, and the caring experience of truly being seen, heard, and supported.

Join
Become an ally for your children. Pay attention to their lives. Know their interests, their friends, their fears, and their challenges. Spend time together. Listen and take their side. Let them know you are there

for them. I recently observed a poignant example of a parent validating and joining with his son. In the parking lot of the health club, I followed a mom, dad, daughter, and son heading to their car. Mom was clearly quite upset, her anger radiating off her in waves. She turned to her son, who was walking with dad behind her, and said something hurtful to him. I couldn't hear the words, but the affect was clear—she made a direct hit. The boy, who looked to be around nine or ten, hung his head and slowed his pace. After a couple of steps, dad reached out and laid his hand on his son's back, and kept it there as they walked. This simple, comforting gesture spoke volumes. "I see you," it said. "You're not alone."

Listen
One of the most valuable gifts we can give another human being is to deeply listen. This means offering our full awareness, where we aren't formulating what we're going to say next, where we aren't giving advice or criticism, where we aren't turning the conversation back to ourselves, but where we open our hearts and minds to what is being said. We simply receive what they say, in an environment of safety. The more you listen, the more your children will tell you.

Get Better at Communication
In healthy, effective communication, there is a sender and a receiver, each with an important role. For communication to work, there must be connection—what is sent must be received and what is received must be acknowledged. This may sound terribly basic, but in reality, effective communication takes some practice. If you are the sender, craft statements that are clear, direct, and kind. Don't expect the other person to *figure out* or *intuit* what you mean through mind reading. If you are the receiver, let the sender know that you heard what was said. This can be a nod, a smile, a verbalization, or a direct response. Each time you talk with your children you model communication skills, and this is how they learn. In these ever-present interactions, you have multiple opportunities to teach your children to be good senders and receivers, to name their feelings, to be assertive rather than aggressive, and to work through problems and find solutions.

Rebuilding

And when you blow it, like everyone does now and then, be sure to go back and rebuild the connection. Here's how rebuilding might sound. "You know this morning when you were trying to tell me what you needed for your science fair project? I snapped at you that we didn't have the money for such an elaborate plan." Your child nods, remembering. "Well, I am so sorry for discouraging you. I was worried about a big meeting I had at work, and I didn't really listen to you, and I let my worries get in the way. I know you are really interested in doing this exhibit. I'd love to hear more about it. Maybe we can figure out a compromise to make it more affordable." In this interaction, Mom takes responsibility for her part in the disconnected communication. And then she reconnects by asking more about the project and validates her son's interest in the science fair. It's a big repair job that only took a few minutes to achieve.

Spend One-on-One Time

Find times when you can be alone with your children, sometimes together and sometimes with each child alone. This provides you the opportunity to really tune in to that child, show them direct attention, and build individual connections. Think of it as the most beautiful gift you can give. Children experience your time as love. These one-on-one times are so important. Get creative about how to make them happen. They don't always have to be big events. Even a quick outing for ice cream or to buy new shoes count. This may look like a daunting task because you want to be perfect and yet you know that you aren't. Take a quick breath and show yourself some compassion. We don't expect you to be perfect communicators. In fact, that's a pretty unreasonable expectation because perfect is way too hard to achieve for most of us. All we suggest is "good enough." Keep at it. Your efforts at improving your communication skills serve as a model for your children to do the same. Responsive parenting is an ongoing set of small, consistent actions that you do to let your children know that you are there for them and they can count on you. These actions create emotional safety and security that help your children thrive.

~

CHAPTER ELEVEN

Help Your Children Develop Self-Compassion

In chapter 8 we talked about the difference between self-worth, which is based on comparison to others, and self-compassion, which is kindness toward oneself, and promised techniques you can use to help your children learn to be more self-compassionate. We likened self-compassion to an apple, solid on the inside, able to withstand many things that may cause it stress, in contrast to the balloon-like qualities of self-esteem—somewhat fragile and easily popped.

What Self-Compassion is NOT

While self-compassion might seem to be nothing more than a self-indulgent "feel good" approach, nothing could be further from the truth. A growing body of research supports the positive results of practicing self-compassion and disproves many erroneous beliefs that have kept people trapped in an endless loop of judgment and self-criticism. Kristen Neff, PhD[1] describes five of these myths that have been debunked by research.

- Self-compassion is a form of self-pity.
- Self-compassion is just being weak.

- Self-compassion lets a person off the hook and creates complacency.
- Self-compassion is another form of narcissism.
- Self-compassion is being selfish.

These are not accurate statements about self-compassion. Far from it. Learning to approach life's many challenges with kindness toward yourself is one of the best gifts you can give yourself, and ultimately your children.

What Self-Compassion Really Is

Before we get into *how* to develop self-compassion, let's review the definition along with the benefits. Self-compassion is learning to pay attention to what's happening in the present moment. It is accepting our thoughts, feelings, and bodily sensations without judgment. It comes from understanding our common humanity with one another—that we all struggle and don't always know what to do. At the core of self-compassion is recognizing our connection to each other, our struggles and vulnerabilities as we practice more kindness toward ourselves.[2] If we reduce the definition to one profound sentence, it's this:

Self-compassion is quieting the inner critic and recognizing that no matter what is happening in our lives, we are still worthy and lovable.

Many years ago, I (Jean) attended a parenting workshop where the speaker placed a paper sign attached by a string around his neck, like a placard. On it were written the words, "I am loveable and capable." He went on to describe how each of us puts on this sign, though invisible, at the beginning of each day and then heads out into the world. Little by little, through the course of the day, bits of the sign are torn off, until by the day's end, we are left with nothing but the string dangling around our neck. It was a memorable demonstration. Now, all these years later, and informed by the research from numerous studies of self-compassion, I realize that the ongoing practice of self-compassion helps us reattach the bits of our sign that events of the day tear off. This example is a visual demonstration of the power of self-compassion. I sometimes envision self-compassion as an efficient team of street workers continually repairing potholes, broken signs, and cracked sidewalks so that I can make my way in life with greater ease.

Self-Compassion and Well-Being

Dr. Richard Davidson, a leading researcher in the field of neuroscience, says that self-compassion lies at the heart of well-being.[3] The benefits of self-compassion are huge.

- reduced anxiety and depression
- less shame and/or embarrassment when things don't go well
- steadier, more consistent sense of self-worth that carries into adulthood
- stronger overall coping skills
- greater well-being
- compassion for others

Setting the Stage for Self-Compassion

There are several important aspects of self-compassion as a practice that may help as you ponder how to help your children develop self-compassion.

Self-Compassion Starts with You

First, you must be compassionate with yourself. This may sound so obvious that it is almost funny. But when you look beyond the obvious you are likely to find that practicing self-compassion isn't as easy as you may have thought. For hundreds of years, our culture has believed and supported the myths, mentioned earlier in this chapter, that self-compassion is self-indulgence, self-pity, or the height of entitlement. As a culture, we have believed that the best way to motivate people is through criticism. NOW we know that is absolutely untrue. As you begin to practice self-compassion, remember it's like learning anything new. It takes time and practice and honestly, some days will be easier than others. There will be days when you won't be able to be self-compassionate at all. Just keep at it. This on-again-off-again experience simply confirms that you are human.

Modeling Self-Compassion for Your Children

Being compassionate with yourself, instead of being critical, is the most effective way to teach your children. Much as we hope our children will listen to our words and learn from them, they tend to learn most from our actions. So, when you drop a glass as you are putting it into the dishwasher, it's a perfect teaching opportunity. You might say aloud, "How could I be so clumsy? Stupid me. Now I have to spend money on a new glass." Or you could take a much more compassionate approach and say something like, "Wow that wet glass was really slippery. I'll just clean it up so no one gets cut. We can get by without it for a while until I can get to the store." Do you see the difference? The second example is much kinder. It also offers a plan of action and a tone that says, "I've got this." It's much easier to replace a glass than it is to repair a psyche.

As you develop your own practice of self-compassion, you will find yourself in a much stronger and more resilient position to deal with your relationships at work, with friends, family, and your spouse, all the while serving as a model for your children.

Self-Compassion Is a Skill

It's helpful to know that self-compassion is a skill that anyone can learn. We are never too young, too old, too set in our ways, or too damaged to develop a practice of self-compassion. All it takes is time and consistency and the willingness to keep at it.

Small, Frequent Steps

Research shows that we humans learn best through small, incremental experiences repeated many times. As author and family therapist Linda Graham, MFT, says, "little and often"[4] is much more effective than trying to learn something in one gigantic step. That means each time you respond to a situation with self-compassion you are strengthening that response in your brain. And as your children observe your compassionate response, they strengthen their own neural pathways for self-compassion.

Emotions Are Contagious

We tend to easily pick up emotions from each other—all of them. Think about a time when you were around a very happy person. Chances are good that your mood was lifted too. And conversely, when someone in the family is in a bad mood, stomping around the house, glowering and complaining, it can affect how everyone feels. In NP/BP dominated families this is likely to be a frequent occurrence. Key to protecting against this emotional contagion is developing healthy emotional boundaries that allow you to discern which emotions belong to you and which do not. Just because one person in the family is upset doesn't mean that you have to own the same emotion. This process of emotional discernment takes some practice, but it is well worth the time and is another significant gift you can give your children.

When you first wake up in the morning, check how YOU are feeling. This is the most likely time that your feelings are entirely of your own making. Then, periodically take time throughout the day to check on what you're feeling. Notice what differences happen throughout the day. Have you picked up hurt or anger from the NP/BP, or pain or frustration from your children? Take a moment to let those feelings go back to their owners, and, instead, tune in to what is going on just for YOU. This helps you keep clear boundaries between your energy and the energy of others.

Self-Compassion Is Especially Important in NP/BP Dominated Families

Every family can benefit significantly from learning to address and ease life's challenges with a practice of self-compassion. You are likely reading this book because yours is a NP/BP dominated family. That means you have a critical role to help our children develop the kind of emotional agility and self-compassion that will carry them through the emotionally turbulent times. You are likely to be the primary model of self-compassion for your children, so keep it high on your agenda every day.

Help Your Children Develop Self-Compassion

In the following steps to help your children develop self-compassion, keep the "little and often" phrase in mind. It will help you feel less overwhelmed, that you must do it perfectly and all at once. Learning to be kind to ourselves is an ongoing process, and as we said earlier, there will be good days and not so good days. Every day that is less than perfect is just one more opportunity to practice self-compassion. Here are some ideas to put into practice with your children.

Model Compassion and Self-Compassion

In the words you use and the actions you take, ensure that compassion for others and self-compassion is a value that you demonstrate. Let your children see and participate in your acts of compassion for others. For example, you might invite them to help you make cookies for a friend who's having a rough time, or organize a snow-shoveling afternoon for an elderly neighbor. Talk with your children about why you are taking the cookies or shoveling the walks so they understand the joy of giving and helping out others.

Freely Give Tender, Loving Compassionate Care—TLCC

Treat your children with kindness. Use positive words in your interactions with them. Appreciate your children as individuals, and be open and supportive of their unique personalities. When you've said something sharp to a child, make an effort to go back and repair the rift.

Here's an example. on a weekday morning when you are rushing to get to work for an important meeting and your five-year-old son is dawdling over getting his shoes on so you can get out the door on time, you lose your patience and snap at him. "You are such a slow poke. Can't you see I'm in a hurry? Now get going or I'll take you to school without your shoes." This interaction is likely to end in tears and more frustration for both of you.

When your emotions have calmed and you are able to talk, perhaps in the car on the way to school, or later in the day, you can go back to the conversation and do some self-compassion-building repair work. "I want to talk about what happened this morning when I yelled at you. I called you a slow poke and it hurt your feelings. And I said I was going to take you to school without your shoes, which would be a terrible experience for you. I'm so sorry I said those things to you. You are not a slow poke. You were just having a slow start to this particular day. Everyone has days like that. I was having a stressful start to my day because I had a very important meeting at work, and I was nervous about it. I took my nerves out on you, which made you feel bad. I'm very sorry for yelling at you. Sometimes grownups have hard days and say things they regret."

In this example the parent does a good job of repairing the rift. She apologizes and reframes her child's story. "You're not a slow poke," she says. "You were just having a slow day. Everyone has those." These words let her child know that he is like every other human being who sometimes has a slow day. And then she models doing the same for herself.

Point Out Compassion in Others

Help your children notice acts of compassion, and particularly acts of self-compassion in books, movies, television programs, and music. Start a conversation about what was said or what action was taken. Discuss how it made others feel. Broaden your conversation to include examples that are not compassionate. For example, you may be watching a movie together in which one of the characters calls another person a loser. This is a great time to talk about how those words felt to the person being called a loser. You might even extend the discussion to something that happened to you. "You know sometimes when I've made a mistake, I'm tempted to tell myself that I'm a loser. My high expectations get in the way of me being kind to myself. But what I know is that everyone makes mistakes now and then. It has nothing to do with the kind of person they are."

Loving Kindness Meditation

Many self-compassion teachers make use of something called the Loving Kindness, or Metta Meditation, with children. This meditation consists of silently repeating four phrases that are like making wishes for our own well-being and for the well-being of others. You can easily teach this meditation to your children. Author and yoga teacher Gail Silver[5] suggests that this meditation practice "creates a warm-hearted feeling within us, and elevates our capacity of self-compassion and benevolence. This pleasant effect can be immediate, but more often arises subtly, manifesting in our everyday life as contentment and a renewed appreciation for other people." She suggests that we can use it to inform and soften our lives as well as the lives of our children. To teach your child this meditation, sit together and suggest she close her eyes and take a few deep breaths, paying attention to how the breath feels as it goes in and out of her body. After a few breaths, begin with the first of the four phrases:

- May I be happy.
- May I be safe.
- May I be strong.
- May I be peaceful.

Next go through the same four phrases about someone she loves:

- May he be happy.
- May he be safe.
- May he be strong.
- May he be peaceful.

Next comes saying the same phrases for someone who is difficult. And last, offering the phrases for all beings everywhere.

Research shows that practicing a Loving Kindness Meditation along with the accompanying deep breathing has eighteen science-based benefits,[6] including decreasing negative emotions, decreasing chronic pain, increasing empathy, compassion, and resilience, reducing self-criticism, and improving self-compassion. The Loving Kindness Meditation is effective in small doses and has a long-term effect. With so many positive benefits, Loving Kindness is definitely an asset to place in your parenting toolbox.

Help Change Your Children's Perspective
If they say something hurtful about themselves, you might ask, "If this were happening to one of your friends, what would you say to him? I bet you wouldn't say something unkind. You would probably be encouraging and helpful. Right? So now you get to practice being a friend to yourself and use the same kind and encouraging words."

Give Your Children Words for Their Feelings

Name it. Claim it. Let it go. Help them talk about feelings. Don't discount or ask them to feel better before they are ready. Here's an example. Your seven-year-old daughter is playing ball with you in the backyard. She is getting silly and tosses the ball to you without paying attention, and it hits you in the head, hard enough to hurt. "Hey, watch what you're doing. That one hurt me," you say. She responds by slamming the ball down and running into the house. You find her sitting on the couch, crying. "I'm a terrible girl," she repeats. "I'm never playing ball again."

Here's your self-compassion moment. You sit close to her and put your arm around her. "You didn't mean to hit me in the head. We were having fun and you were trying out silly moves, right? I bet it surprised you as much as it did me when that ball hit my head." You both take a deep breath. "It sounds like you felt embarrassed and worried that you'd hurt me," Maybe she nods in agreement, or just listens, so you continue. "Things like this happen to all of us in one way or another. Mistakes are part of being human. You were trying something new and it just didn't work like you thought it would. That's all. It has nothing to do with you being a terrible girl. Nothing at all."

Gently Challenge Catastrophic Thinking

When a situation doesn't go well for your child, he might make a catastrophic statement like, "I'm just a loser. I can never do anything right." This is your opportunity to help him see things in a different way. Much like the previous example, you can reframe your child's statement, sort of like editing a story. You could even use that metaphor. "Let's tell this story with a different ending." Then you proceed to help your child create a new story.

Get into the drama of it. "Once upon a time there was a boy named Jason who really, really wanted to (you fill in the blank with the appropriate situation). He did this and this (again use specific examples), but it didn't work. He was so very disappointed. He thought not getting this meant he was a loser. But he was wrong. What it did mean was that he tried hard for something he wanted, and trying is a valuable skill to have. Now he knew more about (the situation) and could try again if he wanted. Or he could decide to do something entirely different. It took him a while to figure out that trying and not getting something has nothing to do with who he is as a person. And that was the best skill of all. The end." Once you make up a new story you can have a conversation, or many conversations, about all of the options.

This chapter has presented several suggestions for ways to develop self-compassion in children. Helping your children become more self-compassionate is an important parenting task and one that will make a huge difference in their lives as well as your own. The research-based benefits are significant. The most effective way to teach self-compassion is to model it in your words and actions. Little and often is best. Self-compassion is a skill that anyone can learn at any age.

CHAPTER TWELVE

~

Help Your Children
Have Their Own Lives

In the narcissistic family system, there is typically only room for the interests of the NP/BP parent. Everyone else is expected to share the same interests, though never at a level to outshine the parent. Here's an example: ten-year-old Jessica is smitten with ballet. She loves everything about it and wants nothing more than to take lessons at the local dance studio. Her narcissistic father demands that instead of dance, in which *he* has no interest, she should follow in his footsteps and play baseball, even though she couldn't care less about the sport. He refuses to encourage her passion and pay for ballet. "We are baseball people," he tells her. "What will people think of me if you break our family streak?"

From this interaction and many others like it, Jessica learns the painful lesson that her interests don't matter. And if her interests don't matter, it isn't a big leap for her to come to the devastating conclusion that *she* doesn't matter. One of the deepest childhood wounds occurs when a child is not truly seen or valued as a unique individual. Because there can only ever be one star in a narcissistic family, children are relegated to the single task of making their narcissistic parent look good at all times.

In contrast, nurturing family environments allow and encourage children to pursue their own interests, even when they don't necessarily continue with them long term. Childhood is naturally a time of exploration and trying ideas and activities on for size. As the non-NP/BP parent, it will mainly fall to you to validate your children's developing interests and activities. It's through your loving support that they will begin to figure out who they are and what makes them tick. In this chapter we'll present a number of ways for you to help your children begin the process of developing their own skills and interests that will ultimately help them grow into competent, independent adults.

Encourage Friendships

Narcissistic families are often marked by rigidity, secrets, and shame, and thus are at risk to becoming a closed system, resistant to outside influences. This creates a stifling, unilateral environment where children are unable to thrive. The more opportunities you are able to provide for them to interact with a variety of family configurations, the better. Through friendships and shared activities, your children can see that there are many ways to be a family, instead of just the one in which they live.

Friendships are much more than simply having someone to play with. Childhood friendships play a key role in social and emotional development. Interacting with friends provides ongoing experiences in problem solving, navigating differences of opinion, resolving disagreements, compromise, listening, and learning the value of loyalty and compassion. Friends become an automatic support system and lifeline when children need to escape the chaos, and the adults, in their family.

Childhood friendships go through developmental stages. Preschoolers tend to do best with one or two playmates at a time, and still engage in parallel play where they play alongside each other rather than doing much interacting. You can facilitate these early friendships by organizing and/or participating in play dates, and scheduling one-on-one meetings with another parent and child at a park or other location.

Elementary school–age children are more comfortable with several friends at a time. They learn to navigate these more complex interactions, enjoy pretending to be grown up, practicing practical skills as well as learning to compromise, share, and take turns. They will make friends at school, from their faith community, in their neighborhood, and in shared sports and other play activities. Your primary task is to lend your interest and support to these new friendships.

Older children are usually well into friend making. Your role with teens is to encourage participation in social events, sleepovers, parties, sports and the like, while keeping your eye on safe boundaries and being an understanding and emotionally safe life skills coach.

Teach and Model Friend-Making Skills

In conversations and by modeling your own behavior in friendships, you help your children learn about what it takes to make and keep friends. This isn't a skill that children automatically have, so parents become their first resource.

John Gottman, PhD[1] found that children who experienced disrespectful, contemptuous behavior from parents demonstrated similar behaviors in their often-unsuccessful attempts at making friends. When there is criticism, belittling, name-calling, sarcasm, and/or humiliating comments aimed at your children by the other parent, it is vital to your children's mental health that you intervene. Give your children hints to reach out to start a conversation with other children, as well as with adults. Give them words to use in an apology. Encourage sharing and helping behaviors.

School and Extracurricular Activities

In addition to being a place to learn, school is an important socialization experience for children. For many families, homeschooling may be an acceptable educational choice, but we don't recommend it for families with a NP/BP parent. The interactions with classmates, teachers, parents, and other staff offer ongoing vital opportunities for your children to observe many different personality styles and have multiple chances to practice their friend-making skills described above. School provides a consistent, predictable, and nurturing venue for your children to explore interests and develop their unique personality styles, free of the criticism and drama that often occur at home.

Outside of the academic and socialization aspects of school, extracurricular activities provide rich experiences for your children to learn about the world around them and receive important feedback that will help them develop. Sports, music, theater, art, theme-based clubs, volunteer experiences, 4-H, and scouts are but a few examples. Tune in to the things that interest your children and pave the way for them to give some things a try.

Support Hobbies and Interests

Childhood is a time of exploration where children try out many different interests. Some children develop an interest or passion early on, and never deviate from it. But it's more likely that your child will "test drive" a variety of things. This is completely normal. Your task as the parent is to support this exploration while also setting loving, clear boundaries. There are always issues of time, finances, and logistics to consider. We are not suggesting that your children try out everything at once or make all of the decisions about what they want while you simply comply. That would create self-centered, overly entitled children. Instead we suggest a cooperative approach that fits your family.

For example, your child may be consumed with basketball. You could help him explore this passion in a variety of ways. You could watch basketball games on television, or attend a local high school or college game together. You could find a beginning camp or team and enroll your child and then attend the practices and games. You could share your own stories of basketball (if you have them). You could get books about basketball from the library and read them together. And then, if/when the interest fades or is replaced with something else, accept it with kindness and grace, knowing it is a perfectly normal part of your child's growth and development.

Attend Events

From infancy on, children seek support and connection from the adults who care for them. Eye contact is an early component in developing secure attachment. Therapist Patti Elledge[2] has coined the term the *beam gleam* to describe the loving eye contact that takes place between parents and their much-loved infants. It is this gaze that says to the baby, "You are so loved. You are special to me. You are safe." Since this gaze experience happens innumerable times in the first few years of a child's life, it lays a critical foundation for developing trust and security.

While your loving gaze is always important to your child's psychological and emotional development, as children get older, they begin to look for another type of connection from their parents. We call this "I contact." It refers to the many ways that parents support their children's interests and activities by attending their various programs, performances, sports, and other events. Children absolutely glow when they look into the stands at an athletic event or the audience for a performance or presentation and see their parents cheering them on. Children will scan the faces of every person attending an event until they locate their parents. Then they seem to relax and continue with the performance. This "I contact" that you give by attending their events is an important way to signal your interest.

A side note to this desire that children have for their parents' loving gaze and attention is that it never completely goes away. Long into adulthood we human beings yearn for and appreciate our parents' support for our events, activities, and achievements. No matter our age, we never lose the desire for our parents to be our own personal cheering squad.

Margalis: For example, on a recent visit with my twenty-six-year-old daughter and her husband, they both asked enthusiastically if I was coming to their recreational kickball game in the park. Of course, I went. It is still a good connection for us.

Maintain Relationships with Extended Family and Friends

It may fall to you as the non-NP/BP parent to make sure your children remain connected to their extended family and friends. Maintaining these relationships gives children a sense of personal community, continuity, and security and is vital to their healthy development. As we said earlier, some families with a NP/BP parent are at risk of becoming a closed system with little or no outside influences. This isn't good for your children. Connecting with extended family members gives your children access to other healthy family members who can be advocates and encouraging support people throughout your children's lives. Schedule celebrations, meals together, vacations, phone calls, and more. As always, keep an eye on healthy boundaries and what's best for your children.

Schedule One-on-One Time

Arrange time with your children without the other parent. When you have more than one child, create times with each child, separate from siblings. We can't stress enough how important it is for you to create pockets of safety away from the drama and tension the NP/BP parent creates within the family. One-on-one experiences with you provide time to talk and listen, time for each child to feel unique and special, and a respite from the household tension and chaos.

These don't have to be costly, time-consuming events. Most busy parents can't manage yet another thing they must fit into their already overcrowded schedule. Instead, think small: a drive together on the way to do an errand; help with a task around the house when it's just the two of you; meet your child for lunch at school; watch a sports practice and then go for ice cream; go for a walk or bike ride together; cook something fun; get out the art supplies or tools and make something. These are just a few ideas. When you think creatively, you can come up with any number of ways for authentic, fulfilling one-on-one time that doesn't break the bank or turn into a scheduling nightmare.

Teach Practical Responsibilities and Independence Skills

One of our primary tasks as parents is to provide a safe and loving environment for our children to grow into competent, caring, self-assured, independent adults. In a sense, everything we do for our children in childhood prepares them to leave home when they are ready. Key to getting our children ready to be on their own is teaching them skills for independence. Much as children would probably not like to hear this, household chores are one of the best ways to develop responsibility and independence. Chores develop a feeling of teamwork and family belonging.

Always keep developmental norms in mind and assign chores that are appropriate to your child's age. An example of reasonable chores for a four-year-old might be taking her plate to the sink, setting the table, picking up toys, and/or helping sort and fold laundry. Older children might be expected to make their beds, feed the pets, clean their room, set the table, take the trash out, and other chores. Middle school children can learn to do their own laundry, cook simple meals, mow the lawn, have regular chores. And high schoolers can use hammer and nails, help organize and clean the garage, be responsible to make their own medical appointments, supervise and transport younger siblings, and have a job outside the home. When children are given tasks that are developmentally appropriate, they feel competent because they know they're contributing members of the family.

Our job as parents is to prepare our children as best we can to head out into the world as confident, competent, compassionate adults. This is ongoing preparation that we undertake every day of their childhood. In a family where there is a NP/BP parent, it becomes even more important to set up opportunities for your children to interact with many families so they see that theirs is not the only kind of family.

Childhood friendships play many important roles in social and emotional development. It is through friendships that children learn resilience, compassion, loyalty, problem solving, conflict resolution, compromise, and fun. In families where there is likely to be drama, tension and chaos, friends are lifelines. The extended family and community can make a significant contribution to your children's self-assurance, understanding of the world, and sense of competence. And their daily and yearly learning to be responsible and contribute to the well-being of the family gives them the confidence to appropriately move into adulthood.

PART III

PARENTING WILL BE DIFFERENT

~

CHAPTER THIRTEEN

What to Say

Handling Family Communication

Mental Illness

Narcissistic and borderline behaviors are symptoms of mental and emotional dysfunction or mental illness. Explaining mental illness to children is difficult in any circumstances, but especially difficult when it involves the child's own parent. Saying that the parent's personality is disordered or disturbed won't make any sense to a child. In addition, there are also many derogatory words used in our culture for mental illness—*crazy, whacko, nuts, eccentric, weird, mad*—which children have heard and can really confuse them.

Not Their Fault

Your goal is to help your children understand that their parent is not acting normally, and it's not the child's fault. Children naturally feel that when a parent is upset, angry, or negative, they are the cause. And too often the NP/BP uses blaming and accusing language when they're angry, intending to make everyone else feel at fault. As children get older, they slowly learn not to take what others say and do as their sole responsibility. However, that requires factual information, practice, and support from you.

You may even find yourself thinking that every negative thing the NP/BP says or does is your fault. So, your first step is understanding that you and your children are *not* the cause of your partner's emotional ups and downs, nor their hostile attitude and comments, nor their distorted and confused thinking. Nor can you or your children heal, fix, or change the other parent's problems.

What to Say
You are the primary source of information and understanding about the hurtful, confusing, and sometimes mystifying behavior and comments of the NP/BP. So, you need to be ready with thoughtful, concrete explanations that your children can understand. Be aware of the language that your children use and match your comments to their level of understanding. It is also best to avoid using labels, diagnostic categories, or slang. Focus instead on describing actual *behaviors* and *feelings*.

Preschool children need to be seen, responded to, and taken care of when the narcissistic/borderline parent becomes emotionally agitated. You could say:

- Daddy's voice was very loud. You are shaking all over. That was scary.
- You just made a mistake. You're not a bad girl. I'll help you fix it.
- That hurt your feelings when mom/dad took your toy away. I'll help you find something else to play with.
- Daddy has mad days sometimes.
- Mom doesn't feel good today. She's very tired and sad.

Middle school children usually need help sorting out the confusion. Here are some examples:

- Mom sure was angry. She's pretty mad at everything today. I'll help you pick up these toys, and then we'll play a game.
- Dad said he'd take you to the game, but he changed his mind. I don't know why, but I know it's not because you did anything wrong. I know you're disappointed. It makes me sad/mad, too, sometimes. What would you like to do instead?

- Dad gets confused and changes his mind a lot.
- I think Mom forgets and asks you to do two things at once. Which do you want to do first?
- Some days Mom/Dad needs to be quiet and alone.

Teens usually know their feelings but need help sorting out what to do.

- Your dad calls you names a lot. I don't like it. How do you feel about it?
- Do you believe what Mom said to you is true? What do you think will help? What are you going to do?
- What help do you need from me?
- When mom is in an angry mood, she doesn't think before she speaks. How does that feel to you?
- Wow, Dad is getting upset at everything today. A good day for us to stay out of the way.
- You're right, your dad didn't keep his promise. I'm sorry he chose not to. I don't understand why. How can I help?

As you can see, keeping your attention on your child and their feelings and reactions are the most effective. Also asking them how they feel and encouraging them to make choices will help them move forward.

Showing how you disagree also can be helpful in expressing empathy. However, outright attacking the other parent to your children can be hurtful to them because they feel connected to that parent and love you both. This can mistakenly lead children to feel a need to choose sides—a choice that is never a win for them.

On the other hand, immediately asserting that the other parent loves the child and didn't mean what they said is both ingenuous and may not even be true. Children need to process what *they* are feeling first. Then it's helpful to distract and remove younger children to a safer and more comfortable environment. Older children can benefit from figuring out what they want to do and then can employ problem-solving skills and effective communication skills to stand up for themselves.

Explaining Ongoing Emotional Dysfunction

We don't recommend ever calling your partner-parent a narcissist or a borderline. If your adult child has done their own research and comes to you saying they think the other parent has BPD or NPD, then be direct and honest with your own assessment. But until then, keep your language focused about behaviors, not labels.

You don't really need to explain mental illness issues to young children other than what we've described previously. However, explanations of ongoing patterns of behaviors can help middle school and older children put things into perspective.

For regularly occurring *narcissistic* behaviors in your partner-parent, you could say:

- Dad often feels scared, and he wants to be the boss so he can feel better. And that can be unfair and hurt your feelings.
- Mom sometimes needs a time out so she can get over being angry.
- Dad wants to make all the decisions. He needs to always feel he's right. He gets really anxious when anything is unexpected.
- Mom feels uneasy when she has to meet new people, so she tries too hard and can become loud and the center of attention.
- You're right. Dad plans out in his mind how everything should go, and when it doesn't go that way, he can get very upset.
- Mom's reasons don't always make sense to anyone else.

For the behaviors of a *borderline* parent, try these:

- Mom gets a lot of very bad headaches. She needs to be quiet and alone today.
- Dad's anger can be scary for all of us. He can't seem to control it. He doesn't have a shutdown switch.
- When Mom's having a good day, it's nice to be around her. But it's best to stay away on her bad days.
- Yes, Dad can't always act the way we'd like him to. His thinking can get very confused, and then what he says isn't true.
- You didn't cause Mom to get sad/mad/upset. Sometimes her mind just makes her feel that way.

Strategies That Help

Stay Vigilant and Aware

Be open and available to talk with your children. Listen to their comments, worries, impressions, and views of the world. All of these give you information about how they are understanding the relationships in your family. Observe their interactions with other children and with your partner-parent. Be ready to help them sort out facts from the delusions the other parent may be presenting. Empathize with their feelings, and give them tools to respond.

Respond, Empathize, Reassure

Make it easy for your children to talk with you. If you're busy and can't listen at the exact moment, tell them when you will be available; for example, "I'm making dinner right now. I want to hear what you have to say. Let's talk right after dinner."

Listen to their thoughts, opinions, experiences, feelings, wishes, and dreams without judgment. This encourages them to be open and at ease. If you child says something that seems impossible or concerning—for example: I'm going to the moon, I'll never eat peas again, I hit Jamie at recess today—don't instantly disagree or reprimand. Instead lead them into more discussion:

- How will you do that?
- Tell me more about that.
- How did that happen?

Start your response with how, when, where, or what to open up the discussion. Avoid responses such as *you should, ought to, can't,* or *don't,* which will immediately shut down the discussion. Empathy brings your children closer, while judgment shuts them down. Here's an example of good listening and responding:

Aaron

Aaron is five years old, his parents are divorced, and he has just come home from a visit with his narcissistic father.

Aaron: "Mommy, today I saw daddy's good side."

Mom: A couple of days later I could tell Aaron was thinking about something, I said, "I know you had a good visit with daddy. How are you feeling about it now?"

Aaron: "It wasn't how he normally acts."

Mom: "What do you mean?"

Aaron: "He's usually not very happy, but this was a really good day."

Mom: "Well, there are good parts to everyone, and not-so-good parts too. I'm glad you got to see some of the good parts of daddy."

Aaron: "Yes. I guess there's a little bit of good in the bad and a little bit of the bad in the good."

Your children will probably need more reassurance that they're OK and you're OK than other children. Showing them that you're confident in yourself and in them will really help. Comments such as, "I think you can figure this out. You've done well before. It's hard but we can do this together," are reassuring. Keep an eye out, and give them a nudge when they need support by offering encouragement and suggestions when they get stuck. Don't jump in and rescue them unless it's clear they can't cope with a situation themselves.

Let Go of Feeling Sorry or Guilty

It's very common for parents in your situation to feel guilty for choosing the partner that you have, and then feeling sorry for what you're "putting your children through." First of all, it's highly unlikely that you knew your partner had these emotional issues and disabilities before you committed. The NP/BP's difficult behaviors don't usually show up until they're in an ongoing, long-term relationship. Second, you now have a child together, and that is never going to change. Therefore, figuring out how to handle the situation is far better than self-criticism, anger, or dissolving into pity. And third, your sorrow and guilt will only get in the way of making good judgments in the present.

When you feel sorry for your children, you'll have a tendency to lower your expectations, bend the rules, and give in to their whining and anxieties, instead of helping them face difficulties with courage.

Children are very emotionally observant and responsive, and they'll pick up that they can play on your sympathies. As we noted in chapter 3, this can easily encourage the mistaken goals of attention-seeking, power, revenge, and helplessness.

Sort Out Adult-Child Boundaries

It can be hard to figure out where the adult-child boundaries should be in your home. You'll often be partnering with your children to meet their needs—sometimes even in opposition to the other parent. You'll be talking to your children about feelings, while often avoiding those conversations with your partner. So, where do you draw a boundary?

Definitely encourage your children to talk about their feelings. Sharing your feelings with them is more complex. You want to be helpful and not make things scary and upsetting for them. Too often your opinions and reasons can get mixed up with your feelings in a conversation. To help you sort out what is a feeling and what is too much information—TMI—here are some examples:

TMI: Your Dad makes me so mad.

Feeling: I'm angry right now.

TMI: Your mom just spent all the grocery money and now we have nothing.

Feeling: I'm worried right now, but I'll figure it out.

TMI: I just found out your Dad is having an affair.

Feeling: I'm sad right now, but I'm working on feeling better.

You'll notice that the feeling statements are very simple with no reasons or explanations given. You can also include a reassurance to your child that you're capable of working to feel better. The adult information in the TMI examples shouldn't be shared with your children. It's often frightening to them, and they really don't understand what it means to you or for them. In addition, they can't do anything about those problems.

When deciding what information about the other parent's behavior to share with your children, you'll need to carefully contemplate whether that information would be *useful* or *helpful* to your children. Ask yourself:

- Will the information make my children feel better?
- Will it help them make better choices?
- Will it help them feel stronger or be more compassionate?
- Does the information contain adult content—especially about money, sex, divorce, self-harm, or harming others?
- What do I hope my child will do with the information I'm sharing?

Share your adult information and problems with other adults, such as a good friend, therapist, or lawyer. Work on the problem with your partner out of the earshot of your children. Keep adult issues between adults.

Unhealthy versus Healthy Comments

It's also harmful to your children when you label or describe the other parent in highly negative terms; for example, "Mom's crazy. Dad's a jerk. What an idiot." These comments are your opinions and conclusions, not facts and not feelings. They're highly inflammatory and detrimental for your children to hear. If you get attacked by the NP/BP with name-calling, don't attack back. That just escalates the problems. Instead, state the behavior and your feeling, then take action. Try to follow these steps:

1. *When* I hear name calling/loud voices/angry words, and so on.
2. *I feel* hurt/unhappy/angry. I can't think then. I'm at a loss to respond.
3. *I'll need* to take a walk/take some time out/find somewhere quiet to think this through.

This pattern of responses works well with adults and children and helps deescalate the situation.

Yes, boundaries are complicated in your family, but keep focused on your values, goals, and what you want your children to learn. Be a model for them. And work to help them cope, understand, and feel safe.

Communicating About Change

People with narcissistic/borderline features do best with long-standing customs and patterns, and they have a hard time dealing with any kinds of change. However, children are constantly growing and changing and require new rules, schedules, and responses, which can easily throw NP/BPs out of their comfort zone.

Calmness, determination, and repetition will be important when communicating with the other parent about the children's changing needs, new schedules, expanded limits and boundaries, and even new rules and responsibilities. Don't expect your partner to see the need for the changes or be necessarily cooperative and agreeable to them. Often you and the children will figure out what needs changing and make that decision rather than you and the other parent.

The challenge is sticking with the change and following through until the NP/BP eventually becomes accustomed to the change. Even simple adjustments like soccer is on Mondays now instead of Thursdays can be highly unsettling to your partner-parent. It may trigger them to anger, passively "forgetting," and continuous griping to you and the children. Keep following through with the new patterns until the other parent relaxes, without giving in and without fighting back or being defensive.

The Value of AND

Acknowledge the other parent's feeling and attitudes matter-of-factly, AND state the new information; for example, "I know that changing the night for soccer is a real inconvenience for you, AND (not but) it is now on Monday." Don't get pulled into an argument, or try to explain why the change occurred. Just keep repeating your statement. You can help your children by saying: "Dad has a hard time making changes. It can take him a while to get used to a different night for soccer. It's not your fault. He'll eventually get used to it."

Sticking to facts, staying calm, not being defensive, and lots of repetition will slowly help the other parent become accustomed to these normal changes, and will model for your children how to communicate with the other parent. Giving in to the NP/BP because you think it will keep the peace or stop the complaining will, instead, actually reinforce their distress and make further communication more difficult.

As your children observe you, they'll learn to use the same patterns. And of course, you can give them these same suggestions and prompts to help them communicate more effectively.

Be Kind to Yourself

You have a lot on your plate. However, it won't help for you to become overwhelmed and collapse or explode from the stress. Taking good care of your physical and mental health is essential and an excellent way to model good self-care to your children. Tell your children how you take care of yourself when you're feeling sad, angry, or hurt. Let them see you relaxing, playing, hanging out with friends, and enjoying yourself. Identify what makes you feel grateful. Research shows that gratefulness is energizing and combats stress.[1] Connect with friends on a regular basis. See a therapist for support. Exercise and eat well, and especially get plenty of rest.

Problem Solving

You've already discovered that problem solving in your family is complicated. You partner may or may not be able to help you solve parenting or even daily problems depending on their level of motivation, rationality, or emotionality at the time. You'll often find yourself trying to solve every problem that comes up entirely on your own. Trying to imagine every contingency and disagreement your partner may have and trying to find a solution for it is exhausting and anxiety producing. Instead, ask yourself these questions:

What is the problem? The more you learn to read the emotional fluctuation patterns in your partner and the better you know what your children feel and need, the quicker you can assess problems that come up.

Who owns the problem? Who's upset? The person who is the most demanding that there is a problem is the person who will be most motivated and able to solve it. Look to that person to figure out the solution—even if it's you—and with your help if necessary.

What solution do I think will work? Don't wait for someone else to come up with a solution to the part of the problem that is concerning you. Start brainstorming ideas of how you can solve your concerns and preferences. Encourage your children to come up with ideas to solve their issues as well.

What can I do about it? When you have a list of ideas, consider which ones you can actually do and what resources you have or need. Figuring out what actions you will take is far more effective than convincing someone else to fix things for you.

What help do I need? Resources include money, time, help from others, inner strength, maybe some new skills, or a new perspective. If you don't currently have the resources you need, start working on getting them.

What is my decision? Once you've thought through all these steps, it's time to take action. One decision or action may solve things. However, more likely, there will be a number of steps needed to solve the problem. Prioritize and get started.

Review—Try it out. Reflect. Adjust. At each step, pause and reflect on the results. Are you headed in the right direction? Are you getting the results you want? Is it more costly, or is it easier than you thought? Did you find out more information that leads you to change course? What adjustments do you want to make? Without criticizing yourself or others, make the changes needed and move on.

Example:
Your son wants to join the high school basketball team.
Problem: He needs money for a uniform and he needs to stay at school until 6 pm.
Owner of the Problem: Your son is the most motivated.
His Solution: You give him money and pick him up at 6 pm.
Your Solution: You'll pay half, but you can't pick him up. You have things to do at home at that time.
Son's Resources: He has some savings, but not enough. His friend on the team lives down the street.
The Help You Can Offer: He can help you with a project at home to pay his half, and you suggest that you and the friend's parent can trade off picking both boys up.
Son's Decision: He accepts your offer. You agree.
Review: You find that it's too hard to do the carpooling. Son is too busy to do the help at home that you asked. He's now on the team.

New Issue: Son finds a new person to pick him up. You and son renegotiate how he can pay off his share of the cost.

Teaching your children to solve their own problems, with your help, is an extremely valuable lesson they will use for the rest of their lives. It also allows you to see situations as dilemmas to be solved rather than feeling like a police officer and judge enforcing rules and handing out sentences. Instead of saying yes or no to requests, give your children and your partner the issue to solve—being there to help when necessary.

How you say things in your family will make a huge difference. Giving up and saying nothing or conversely trying to control everything in the family will never work to anyone's advantage. You are the voice of reason for your children. It's important that you use your voice with care and accuracy to help your children learn to stay in reality even when everything around them may be in an uproar. You can do a lot to help them make better sense of the chaos and confusing behaviors in their home. You can model for them healthy ways to think, feel, and respond. You can offer them nurturance, sanity, and support for what they feel and who they are. It takes vigilance, patience, strength, and skill, but you know your children are worth it.

CHAPTER FOURTEEN

~

What Not to Say or Do

Communication in your family can be fraught with difficulties. The NP/BP can be touchy and willing to fight over the slightest thing that you say. Always trying to please and appease her/him, however, will tend to give the NP/BP license to demand unlimited control over every aspect of the family's life and atmosphere. Of course, it also doesn't work to fight over everything either. It works best to pick your battles based on your values and what you believe is best for the children and the family as a whole. The following are suggestions about what we believe are important issues.

Don't Use Your Children as a Sounding Board

Your situation is unique, and you may often feel very alone in your relationship and as a parent. You may often feel frustrated, angry, and hurt, and you may believe that there's no one to talk to who will understand. It can be tempting to make hostile, demeaning comments about the NP/BP to your children or even ask them for advice about what you should do. We encourage you to talk to a friend, therapist, or supportive family member instead.

Even therapists need a team to decompress and support them when they're treating someone with NPD or BPD. Trying to cope with all of the drama and uproar alone can quickly lead you into depression and anxiety. At the same time, you need to be strong and calm, in spite of everything, in order to make good decisions and take care of your children. Keep paying attention to the boundaries you need to maintain with your children, but also get the help and support you need to stay healthy yourself.

Don't Encourage Your Children to Take Sides

It's important to realize that your children's experiences with the NP/BP parent are very different than your own experiences with him or her. The NP/BP interacts as a parent differently than as a spouse or partner, and your conflicts with the NP/BP aren't necessarily the same things that bother your children. In addition, children are often able to take the good and ignore the bad. Try to see your needs and their needs separately.

No person is all good or all bad. Encourage your children to enjoy their positive interactions with the other parent, while also being aware of when things cross the boundary into hurt or putdowns. Children are genetically and emotionally a mixture of you and the other parent. Any attack you make on the NP/BP will be felt by the children as a condemnation of them as well. Your children's discomfort will also get triggered when the NP/BP belittles or insults you. So, it's important that you not quietly accept demeaning comments from the NP/BP. State clearly to the NP/BP that you won't tolerate that behavior and then disengage. Fighting back or being defensive will typically escalate the interaction, which is a guaranteed loss for you and the children.

Don't Triangulate

Don't send messages by way of your children to the other parent. This is called *triangulation*—that is, a three-way conversation. Sentences that start out with: "Tell your father . . . " or "Tell your mother . . . " will inevitably end with confusion and children feeling they will be in trouble with one or both parents for doing what you ask. If you have messages or information you need to convey to the other parent, do it directly yourself through whatever medium works best—verbal, notes, texts, email, or through a family internet calendar.

Don't Fight with the NP/BP

Fighting with the NP/BP will have no positive results. Nothing gets resolved or changed. And fighting can be quite scary for the children. You can't *make* the NP/BP act, feel, or understand anything differently. The two things you can do that are effective are being assertive and taking new actions.

Being assertive requires you to be calm, firm, repetitive, and committed to what you feel is right. It also usually requires you to be ready to *take action* to actually protect yourself and your children. For example: the NP/BP calls you a fat, lazy bitch. Look him straight in the eye and say, "No, I'm not." Then quietly walk away. Future repetitions of that putdown will only require you to exit, hang up the phone, or refuse to respond. No words are necessary.

The NP/BP starts hitting or screaming at the children. Say, "This behavior is not OK. When you can calm down, we can talk about what needs to be done." Then, take the children to another room or leave the house. When you return, set clear boundaries about not hitting or screaming. Write out the agreement and put it on the refrigerator or somewhere visible. A parent who is not willing to make such an agreement can't be trusted with care of the children.

Don't get involved with haggling back and forth, explaining, or trying to win. Fighting actually feeds the NP/BP's need for your energy and attention. What NP/BPs fear most is that you will leave them or not pay attention to them. So, taking yourself out of the situation is very effective.

Don't Lie, Pretend, or Deny the Truth to Your Children

You may feel that you should never say anything negative about the other parent to the children. However, when they come to you and say the NP/BP is being mean, scary, or doesn't love them, denying their feelings and the facts of the other parent's behaviors will be injurious to your children—making them feel wrong, crazy, or unable to trust their own perceptions. Instead, ask them to tell you what happened and how they felt. Console them, sympathize with their feelings, and ask how you can help.

If your child asks you about your reactions and feelings, be honest, but brief. "Yes, that hurt my feelings. I *am* disappointed. This is not what I expected. No, I don't like being yelled at." This can be done without demeaning the other parent and without dishonesty.

Teach your children words for their feelings so they can accurately assess and understand their world. See Appendix A for a list of feeling words. Don't ignore, discount, or reject what they feel. At the same time, don't join in and feel their pain, hurt, or anger because that will just make those feelings bigger and more overwhelming for everyone. They need to know you understand and will help. They don't want to make you feel like they do. They want you to help them feel strong and safe again.

Don't Blame Your Children for the NP/BP's Reactions

Neither you nor your children are the cause of why the NP/BP acts the way he/she does. It is entirely the NP/BP's own reaction, their own choice, and their responsibility for what they do and say. Speak the truth without blame. "Yes, Dad is very angry right now," instead of "What did you do to make Dad angry?" Also, don't make your children apologize when, in fact, the uproar was caused by the NP/BP. Teaching your children they're responsible for how other people behave will make them vulnerable to choosing and tolerating abusive relationships as adults.

Don't Make Excuses for the NP/BP

Saying that Mom is having a bad day is a fact that can help you and the children choose what to do. But don't use it as an excuse to condone screaming, tantrums, and generally hostile behaviors from the NP/BP. If you exempt adult bad behavior, children won't understand why you expect them to act nice despite having a bad day. They may learn they can't trust your judgment nor believe you are fair or trustworthy. Set boundaries on the behaviors that you will tolerate from the NP/BP and remove yourself and your children from volatile and abusive situations.

Don't Expect Adult Behaviors from the Children

Really observe yourself and your family's interactions to see if you are expecting your children to act more maturely than the adults. Is it acceptable for adults to scream and slam doors, but not for children? Can adults not clean up after themselves, but kids are held to a more rigid standard? Do you send children to their room for anger, crying, or sassing, but the adults get a pass? Can parents break promises, but children are shamed if they do? Do the adults not tell the truth, but children are punished for lying?

These discrepancies don't seem fair or justified to children and will tend to affect their level of trust and sense of fairness in you. Children can become resentful, spiteful, and feel life is against them when things are so inequitable.

Allowing the NP/BP to act childishly while expecting the children to act more maturely needs a real explanation. Children can be very compassionate and understanding of a parent who is disabled. The NP/BP's disabilities are confusing because they blame their behaviors on others. Help your children to recognize that Mom/Dad is not thinking or functioning well in certain situations. This will help them to not take the behavior of the parent as their fault. For example:

- Mom isn't thinking clearly today.
- Dad can't understand other people's feelings very well.
- Mom easily forgets what she says or does from the day before.
- Dad mostly remembers what *he* likes to do, but he's not very good at remembering what *you* like.

Don't Make Promises You Can't Keep

Do you find yourself making promises for or about the NP/BP parent? You may think this is reassuring to your children, but in fact you're teaching them your own delusional beliefs. "Your dad will be there on time. Your mom is going to counseling and everything will be better soon." When these things inevitably don't happen, children again find it hard to trust your words.

Don't Take Your Anger Out on the Children

Life in an NFS can be very frustrating, disappointing, stressful, and exhausting. You may find yourself angry, depressed, fuming, and miserable with no one to help you relax and regroup. It can be very hard not to let these feelings out at your children when they're being disruptive and uncooperative. However, continually stuffing your feelings, denying them, and telling yourself you're wrong to feel as you do will guarantee that you'll head into depression or blow up.

You need to release these feelings in some way. Having a support group, friends, a therapist, or close family members who will listen nonjudgmentally will be essential. You can't deal with an emotionally disabled and distraught person every day without help. You'll always need lots of good sleep, healthy food, and plenty of exercise, massages, or yoga to help you release all of the tension that builds up in your body. When you take care of yourself, you'll find it easier to handle the regular day-to-day stresses of being a parent.

Don't Fall Apart in Front of the Children

Taking care of yourself, refusing to fight with the NP/BP, and lots of support from others can help you avoid falling into panic, anxiety, and/ or deep unhappiness. If your energy or strength collapses, then your children are left with no one to rely on. You are really the anchor for the family. Your reliability, honesty, and validation are essential for your children's well-being. Don't let yourself disintegrate in order to keep up appearances, to make everything work, or to make the NP/ BP happy.

Don't Forget

The NP/BP Does Have Positive Interactions with the Children

The NP/BP in your life has many positive qualities, strengths, and abilities that do contribute to your family. They're not *unable* to function as a parent. They have limitations and areas of disability—especially when they're under stress—but they also contribute a great deal to the family. They can be charming, witty, really good at having fun, and add lots of energy and enthusiasm. They bring in income, provide meals, and do a lot to keep the functions of the family going. They participate in school and community activities. And their intellectual functions are not affected by their personality deficiencies.

Try to keep these positives in mind, while still being observant and ready to step in when necessary. Human beings are very complex, and we are all a combination of multiple facets that function along a continuum. A good strategy is to acknowledge the strengths and limitations of each parent and work out ways to use those strengths for your children's benefit and step in to help when those limitations get in the way.

You're a Powerful Role Model

Children's primary mode of learning is through observation. They have their eyes on their parents, teachers, and other adults as a means to learn as much as they can about how to be a human being. They can learn something new through one observation. The more trusting and emotionally close they feel to you, the more important your actions are for their learning. You're a powerful role model. How you handle situations gives your children valuable and useful information about what they should do and how they should behave. Pay attention to the messages you're teaching them about love, compassion, strength, hope, and honesty. And also pay attention to what you're teaching them about anger, standing up for yourself, and how to handle conflicts.

You DO Have Choices

So many times, over our years of being therapists, we've heard clients say to us, "I have no choice." Our message throughout this book is that you have many, many choices. You constantly choose how you think, what you say to yourself and others, and what actions you take every minute of every day. Even the smallest change in any of these actions can change the results of what happens to you and to your children. Too often, we go through days and weeks without even noticing what we're thinking or doing. However, we're still making choices.

Become more aware of what you're choosing to say and do each day. Are your actions congruent with your values? Are you basing your choices on facts and accurate information, or on what you believe you're *supposed* to think and do? Have you thought through how you want to respond, or are you just emotionally reacting? Are your choices moving you toward your personal and parental goals?

Pick your battles, be aware of your choices, keep your children's best interests in mind, and take good care of yourself. Don't ignore truth, but try not to become overwhelmed. You are smart. You are loving. You are strong.

CHAPTER FIFTEEN

~

Responding to Emotional and Physical Dangers

We have shared ways to teach your children to develop self-compassion and skills to build their resilience and outlined what you can do to create an environment for them to thrive, even within your difficult atmosphere. We know, however, that you can't *control* the behaviors, attitudes, and reactions of the narcissistic or borderline parent. It's likely that you feel your family is always on the verge of the next disaster, and you're right. So, it's important for you to be prepared for the disturbances, distresses, and even dangers that can occur almost out of the blue.

It's very easy to ignore, deny, and discount the truth of your situation. When you see the other parent acting normally, you breathe a sigh of relief, hoping that things are *back to normal.* You may feel that you just want to not rock the boat and put the last uproar out of your mind for a while. However, ignoring the issues that are inevitably going to resurface simply leaves you unprepared and your children facing another disturbing and distressing situation. The only way to keep moving toward the positive environment you want for your children is to be prepared ahead of time to handle the next chaotic event.

You Won't Be Working as a Team

One way you can easily fall into denial is hoping and pretending that you and the narcissistic/borderline parent can work as a team. You're being told by society to work together as parents for the benefit of your children, be on the same page, and present a united front. This cooperation may happen some of the time, but you have to be prepared for when the other parent's behavior gets emotionally unbalanced or threatening, and you need to be able to stand your ground to protect your children. This chapter will offer you ideas and suggestions for doing that in as nonconfrontational and supportive ways as possible. However, there may be times when things get too out of hand, and you'll need to protect your children more forcefully or take them and exit the situation.

If you are pretending that the other parent will never have emotional problems again or, on the other hand, if you're always on edge, angry, and frightened not knowing what will happen next, you can't be really prepared to protect your children. When you're prepared and have a plan, you can enjoy the good times, and have the confidence that you'll quickly be ready to take action when things deteriorate.

Very Little Coparenting

Parenting as a team will mostly be a desire rather than a reality. Assuming that you can intuit from casual conversation how the two of you will approach parenting is unlikely to be satisfactory. Try sitting down together and writing down goals of parenting and basic rules. (Or write these up yourself if the other parent refuses to participate.) Post them in a visible place and refer to them frequently in conversation. When the other parent starts slipping into hostile, demanding, or controlling behaviors, instead of being either outraged or ignoring their behavior, try these prompts instead:

- We've agreed that we want to have a calm and loving atmosphere in our home.
- I can handle this situation with Ariana if she's disturbing you.
- Does the rule you're proposing fit in with our parenting goals?
- How can we work together to help Jeffrey feel good about getting his school project completed?

When you have visible evidence of agreement, it makes you less of an enforcer, boss, or controller. However, there will continue to be times when the other parent will be so emotional that he/she can't contain themselves and will totally ignore any agreements the two of you have previously arranged.

Although there will surely be good times, the emotional problems of the parent with narcissist/borderline characteristics do continue to appear. These are not problems that get significantly better—at least, not during the period of time you'll be raising your children. Pretending that the other parent is going to recover and that you'll be able to be a team can comfort you in the moment, but that leaves you unprepared for the next chaotic event.

Boundaries

When the other parent is calm and rational, you can proceed pretty normally. However, the core problems of the narcissistic/borderline parent—lack of empathy, selfishness, and emotional dysregulation—will continue to crop up. Setting up clear boundaries, that you're prepared to enforce, will be needed to protect your children and yourself. Do you know where your limits are? Do you know what you will and won't tolerate? Do you have protection plans when these limits are not respected by the other parent? At a minimum, boundaries will be needed for hurtful *words*, harmful *behaviors*, and hostile *threats*.

Words do, in fact, hurt—perhaps more than anything else. Children benefit most when there is a ban on name-calling, insults, and spiteful comments from their parents, with their siblings, and in their own use. If a parent is saying hurtful things, it's hard to keep children from picking up the same language. Punishing children for hurtful speech but condoning or accepting the same from the other parent will not provide a safe environment. Stating clearly and emphatically that hurtful, hateful speech is not acceptable and then removing the combatants from each other works pretty well. If you can't moderate the other parent's talk, then at a minimum talk with your children after these events about your attitude toward harmful words, and definitely empathize with their feelings. For example: "It was mean of mom to say those words to you. You don't deserve to hear that. And it isn't true.

I'm sorry I couldn't keep you from hearing that." Then, figure out what to do about it.

Behaviors such as shouting, screaming, throwing or breaking things, and of course, pushing or hitting the children are all too often common behaviors in homes with a narcissistic/borderline parent. These behaviors are abusive, extremely upsetting, and traumatizing to children. If you stand by and let the other parent do these things, hoping they'll calm down soon, your children will assume: 1) You agree with these behaviors. 2) You are powerless to change anything. 3) You can't be trusted to protect them. You must demand that such behaviors stop, and if they don't, you are responsible to remove your children from the situation. If they are physically harmed, in most states, you'll be as liable for allowing the behavior as much as the other parent is for committing the abuse.

Daniel

Daniel was horrified to find out that after he left for work, his wife would scream and call their three children stupid, dumb, useless, and selfish whenever she felt overwhelmed, especially when trying to get them off to school. She would also spank the two youngest girls if they didn't hurry up. He made it clear to the family that name-calling and hitting was against their family rules. However, that reminder worked only sporadically. He talked with the children about how he had heard that their mornings weren't going well. They cried and said they were angry at their mom for yelling and at him for leaving. He decided to take new action. He rearranged his work schedule to go in a half hour later, and he took over getting the children ready for school and out the door. Everyone had a better start to their day.

Stating your positive parenting expectations, modeling those behaviors, and changing the situation are all techniques you can use to protect your children.

Threats from the NP/BP may also be a problem. He or she may threaten dire punishment for disobedience, threaten to leave or get a divorce, threaten to burn the house down, and/or threaten to harm themselves.

Marlena

Marlena said her most vivid memory from childhood, which she and her siblings still talked about, was the night their mother cornered them on the stairway with a butcher knife in her hand. Her BPD mother was screaming for one of them to please cut off her hand because she believed they thought she was a terrible mother. Their only escape was to run upstairs to their bedrooms, shut the door, and hope she didn't follow. Marlena said they never told their father, who wasn't home at the time. They didn't believe he would do anything about it anyway.

Threats of violence can be terribly traumatizing to children. Keeping an open channel of communication with your children can help you know what they're experiencing when you're not around. Then you can help them cope, and you can arrange to change the situation.

Keep the Channels of Communication Open

The best protection you can give your children is to guarantee that you will listen to them, believe them, and take action to make things better. If they're afraid to tell you about their experiences, you may never know about the traumatic interchanges your children have with the other parent when you're not there You want them to know that they can trust you to listen, understand, and help.

Grilling your children or asking them what went on while you were gone, however, will not help. They'll feel intimidated and may feel disloyal for tattling, and they'll clam up. The best times to find out how their lives are going are casual conversations in the car, watching TV, or doing ordinary activities like games, cooking together, home projects, puzzles, reading books, bedtime rituals, and so on. If they feel you're listening, they'll tend to ask questions or make comments that give you a picture of how they're experiencing their world, what they feel, what brings them joy, and what things hurt or scare them. Listen and ask questions to keep the conversation going. Don't lecture, give advice, or get angry.

Stacey

In the middle of getting her hair brushed, nine-year old Jamie asked her mom, "Why is dad so mean to me?"

Stacey asked, "What do you think he's being mean about?"

"He said that learning to shoot baskets is stupid because I'm a girl and I'm too short anyway."

"Do you like playing basketball?" asked Stacey.

"Of course."

"Well, I guess if you like basketball, you could just keep doing it. Don't you think?"

"Yea. But do you think dad believes I'm stupid?"

"You could ask him. What do you think he'd say?" asked her mom.

"Girls are stupid and boys are smart," Jamie says in a deep voice.

Stacey then asked, "Do you believe that?"

"No."

"Well, I guess you and Dad don't agree. I think we girls are pretty darn smart and I know lots of girls play basketball—even on professional teams."

Stacey's conversation with her daughter served to help Jamie think about what she was feeling, what she wanted to do, and what she believed. This helped Jamie a lot more than if Stacey had gotten mad at the other parent and voiced her anger or told Jamie what to do. Instead, she was helping Jamie learn to *not* take a negative comment to heart, while giving her daughter encouragement and strengthening their bond.

Create a Strong, Trusting Bond

Listening, supporting, encouraging, and believing in your children will give them the validation and trust in you that can offset much of the inadequacies of the narcissistic/borderline parent. Being strong enough to protect and support them through the chaotic times will help them build emotional strength and model for them how to stand up for themselves.

When your children tell you their feelings, be sure to listen attentively. Don't ignore, discount, or brush them off. And especially, don't use what they've told you to attack or disparage your partner-parent. Keep their confidences, and consider their feelings when making future decisions. Keep checking back with them to see how they're doing.

Favoritism

It's very common for a narcissistic or borderline parent to latch onto one child as the "favorite" and/or attack another child as a "scapegoat." Both the favored child and the blamed child are in the most danger emotionally of having their inborn sense of self coopted by these inter-actions. In addition, these behaviors put the entire family system out of balance by putting too much of the NP/BP's own ego and neediness onto the selected children. As mentioned earlier, people with these dysfunctional traits tend to merge with their family members and then project their own positive and negative characteristics onto them. This can strongly influence the child's self-image and sense of identity.

Be alert to moving these targeted children out of the attention of the narcissistic/borderline parent. However, be careful of your own tendency to demand too much or overprotect these children. Instead, help them get involved in productive activities with their peers, such as after-school clubs, athletic teams, hobbies, community programs, and even tutoring. These experiences can help them develop their own per-sonalities, interests, and achievements, and provide interactions with a variety of other adult role models.

Become Strategic

The NP/BP gains more control and power over a situation when you feel that you have none. They will criticize you or demean your parent-ing efforts in order to gain power and dominance over you and the chil-dren. You'll need courage and determination to stand up for yourself and the children. In addition, you'll need to develop the ability to see your situation clearly, take effective action, and maintain your sense of control, authority, and potency. Becoming strategic rather than just reactive will be necessary. Being strategic includes:

Diffusing the Situation

Many people believe that validating an NP/BP will make them even more entitled and worse behaved. But there is a very effective way to use validation to diffuse their emotional reactions. Acknowledge and identify their feeling or point of view as real (without agreeing with it) AND then offer a solution or alternative. Here are some examples:

"I can see that the children's noise is bothering you. Let's go outside, kids."

"I understand that having the house in order is important to you. We're all so busy. I'll take care of getting some help."

"Davy, let's move your Legos into your room, so dad can watch the game in quiet."

These examples include validating the feeling of the other parent and offering a solution that you can resolve without the NP/BP's input or help. The validation calms the narcissist/borderline parent while providing a solution, and it avoids encouraging your partner/parent to join in the problem solving. This requires you to assess the problem, figure out a solution, and put that solution into effect. This is much more work for you, but it minimizes the likelihood of a harmful incident with the emotionally overreactive parent. And with practice, it will become second nature.

Redirecting the NP/BP's Attention

Validating the narcissist/borderline is your first redirect, because it moves their attention away from focusing on the children to thinking about themselves. You can then offer an appealing suggestion about where and how they can put their attention onto something they will enjoy more. For example:

"Then you can have some peace and quiet."

"This can give you time to finish what you were doing . . . go out with your friends . . . do that project you were looking forward to . . . etc."

"I'll handle this so you can go on to the gym."

Removing Yourself and the Children

When the NP/BP and the children clash, your goal is to separate them. This allows the other parent to calm down, and it protects the children from the emotional chaos, anger, and irrationality that is being discharged. It requires you to step in with calming language, and then do something with the children away from the other parent. You're essentially giving the NP/BP a strategic time out.

Sometimes the time apart requires just a few minutes. Other times you and/or your children may need to spend hours away or even overnight before things are calm enough to return. Having a list of enjoyable activities to do ranging from going to the park for an hour, riding bikes, visiting the zoo, or just getting ice cream can make the time away for you and the children enjoyable. If a longer time away is needed, the children might visit their grandparents, stay overnight with a friend, or you might even take them on a weekend trip. Also, encouraging the NP/BP to spend time away on things they enjoy can help lower the anxiety, stress, and pressure they so often feel due to the responsibility of parenting.

If one child is being hostilely attacked or extremely enmeshed by the partner-parent, you may even feel the need to find a place for that child to stay for several weeks; for example, for the summer vacation, or half a school year. You'll want to make it a positive experience in a home your child finds comfortable and nurturing, and with no indication that this is *sending the child away*. We highly suggest that you work with a therapist to evaluate the need for this option and to get their help to set it up.

More Time and Energy on Your Part

When you're parenting with someone who has bouts of dysfunction and emotional dysregulation, you will naturally have to take over much more of the parenting duties than if you had a fully functioning partner. This usually requires restructuring your time at work, with friends, and on other activities.

Don't Try to Control the NP/BP

When the other parent is having an overly negative impact on the children, we don't recommend that you try to get him or her straightened out. Trying to fix, control, or force the other parent to behave a certain way or be a better parent will not be successful and will cause more hostility and chaos. Instead, encourage and support any and all positive interactions and diffuse, distract, and remove when negative parenting behaviors come up. It's not your job to retrain your partner-parent. Your job is providing the emotional stability your children need, and protecting them from harm. This does take more vigilance and energy on your part.

Deal with Your Resentment

Most parents in your situation feel at least some resentment about the unfairness of this imbalance in parenting duties. So, you will definitely need to take care of your own emotional and physical well-being. You can't do so much totally alone. You'll need a good support system, which may include: reliable and healthy child care, support of friends and family, a career or work that has some flexibility, community assistance, and dependable finances under your control. You and your children may also need the support of teachers, therapists, and even lawyers and medical professionals.

Get all the information and education you can about the emotional problems that the other parent is bringing to the family system. The more you know, and the more help you can get, the better you'll be able to handle the upheavals and figure out creative and compassionate solutions in response.

In many ways, you and your children will become a team in creating as much of a positive atmosphere as you can. We encourage you to include the other parent when he/she is healthy and functioning. However, be ready to take action when they become emotionally unstable.

When Behaviors Become Extreme

Borderline Dysfunctions

A parent with borderline traits is likely to be vulnerable to episodes of emotional disintegration or collapse. Often these will include the inability to get out of bed, physical pain or migraines, rages, crying, and/or a general inability to go about daily tasks. In those situations, you'll need to be ready to take over complete care of the children and even the household during the time she or he is disabled. This is why flexibility in work hours, schedules, and child care and household assistance can be extremely helpful. These episodes can be sudden and of indeterminate length, so you'll need to have these resources on call. It is also valuable to contact the BP's primary care physician or psychiatrist to set up a medical/psychological visit and evaluation so you can get your partner-parent the help he/she needs.

The situation becomes even more serious if the BP goes into a decompensation episode where they become psychotic and/or threaten harm to themselves or others. Their behaviors can be irrational, frantic, distraught, and so emotionally uncontrolled that the children, and even you, become frightened. During those times, they're likely to talk about, threaten, or attempt suicide. It's unusual for them to purposely try to harm you and the children, but accidents can happen.

As hard as it may be, these are situations in which calling the police may be necessary. When you dial 911, ask for a "mental health check." In many states and communities this will alert the police to send out someone trained to handle mentally agitated people. This usually results in the borderline person being hospitalized for seventy-two hours of observation. The medical staff can then help him/her get on medication to calm them down, and have a chance to come back to reality.

If your partner-parent is not harming or threatening to harm themselves or anyone else and she/he has a psychiatrist, call that person first. They can arrange to see the BP in their office or in the hospital, as is necessary, to continue their care.

Narcissistic Dysfunctions

People with narcissistic behaviors don't usually get so emotionally panicky, frenzied, or withdrawn and unresponsive. Their out-of-control behaviors are typically rages, extreme demands for control, and emotional attacks and threats toward you and the children. Their escalation of these behaviors over time can be insidious, so that you don't immediately notice when they move from name-calling, to insults, to personality annihilation, to contempt, to full-blown emotional threats and/or physical attacks.

If you have ever seen this escalation in your partner-parent, always be prepared to have a plan to get somewhere safe out of the house. Go to safety first, then call 911. Don't tell your partner-parent that you are leaving or where you're going. You may need to distract the narcissist so you can get your children and leave. If he or she is ever violently angry—for example, hitting the walls or breaking things—or has ever threatened or physically harmed you or the children, you need to be prepared to not go back until your partner-parent has gone through anger management and you have concrete evidence that all of you will be safe before returning.

In general, borderline parents collapse and withdraw or physically lash out when they're distraught or emotionally frenzied. Narcissist parents tend to be more belittling, emotionally attack their family members, and are more likely to physically attack in a rage. Because of the possibility of these emotional breakdowns, it is important to NOT have guns or knives accessible or available in your house.

That being said, these extreme behaviors are rare for 95 percent of all parents with borderline or narcissistic characteristics. However, if your partner-parent has ever been hospitalized or arrested for emotional disturbances, you'll need to stay very aware of the red flags and symptoms that indicate an episode is about to happen and be prepared to call 911.

Feeling Alone
In many ways you're likely to feel like a single parent. You may even at times feel like your partner-parent has to be watched and managed like one of the kids. You'll have to be vigilant, strategic, and prepared to handle unexpected changes in the emotional dynamics in your family. This is not an easy job, and you're unlikely to get any praise and appreciation for your efforts. However, this is the situation you're in, and you want to do the best you can to help your children grow to be strong, healthy, productive, and resilient human beings. The suggestions in this chapter are given to help you anticipate and respond in effective ways to accomplish these goals. Even though you'll hopefully never have to call 911 or leave your home in a rush, be prepared for what may happen so you can face your day-to-day challenges with courage, compassion, and a viable plan.

~

CHAPTER SIXTEEN

Assessing Your Situation

Narcissism and borderline disorders occur on a spectrum ranging from some dysfunction to severe dysfunction. Your level of frustration is likely a good indicator of your partner's level of dysfunction, as well as your tolerance for chaos, inflexibility, and hostility. You may find yourself wondering how long you can put up with your relationship situation as it is.

Since you can't make the NP/BP change what he/she does, you've been trying to change how you say things and how you respond. You may find those changes improve your interactions with the NP/BP enough to make it workable, or you may find they don't do enough, or they may be costing you emotionally and physically too much.

Making a clear choice about whether you're going to stay or leave the relationship will help you develop a plan to move forward with hope and conviction. If you plan on staying, then you're looking at more long-term solutions, and it's likely that your partner has fewer disabling behaviors and offers a lot more benefits to the family. However, if you find that you can barely stand to interact with your partner-parent, if you're constantly uneasy and on edge, and you're fighting depression, it's more likely you're considering leaving or you're already divorced and your plan will be to parent your children in different households. There is also a third option. That is, you may choose to stay until the last child turns eighteen, and then you plan to leave your partner. This will remove the need to fight over child custody and child support.

None of these options is easy, and your choice will, of course, depend on your circumstances and the needs of your children. However, knowing that you are the one making the choice can help you through the day-to-day difficulties of parenting with a NP/BP and help you better care for your own mental and physical health.

Two Types of Staying

Long-Term Staying

When your partner has characteristics of NP/BP but a significant amount of the time seems to function effectively both as a partner and a parent, you'll likely feel that the relationship is worth continuing. You may find that learning to set clear boundaries, using direct communication, and being more independent can make the relationship more functional for yourself and the children. It also helps if you're comfortable doing a considerable amount of the parenting and have the time to be attentive to the needs of the children.

Even if you want to stay long term, it's advisable that you have a backup plan to take care of yourself in case the NP/BP has a meltdown or decides to leave the relationship. NP/BPs are unpredictable and impulsive, and they may suddenly do something that is a deal-breaker or just decide to split for their own reasons. We suggest that you have money of your own stored away, a car in your name, and a place for you and the children to stay/live, if necessary.

Being in a relationship long term with a NP/BP means that you'll need to be very attentive to your emotional well-being. Don't discount your feelings and needs, and be sure to find regular and reliable ways to care for yourself. You'll need supportive friends and family members, stress-reducing activities, and plenty of sleep and exercise to keep yourself healthy and mentally strong. Creating your own social connections and activities will really help you to create more balance and independence in your life.

Kyle
Kyle and his wife, Sandy, have been married for ten years and have
three children under the age of eight. Kyle describes Sandy, a stay-at-
home mom, as a good parent and attentive to the children, but she is
consistently hostile and rejecting of him. "She never stops complaining
about how I talk, what I watch on TV, how many hours I'm away from
home." Kyle works fifty to sixty hours a week, which makes a good
living for the family but infuriates Sandy. Sometimes their conflicts
deteriorate into Sandy screaming, threatening suicide, and then being
depressed and nonfunctional for a couple of days. "I actually see that
when I'm not around, Sandy is *better* able to take care of the kids and
our home. And usually we get along pretty well, except for her nag-
ging. So, divorce doesn't seem like the right choice. I couldn't take
care of the children and work. I figure when we don't have so much
stress with the kids, I'll be able to work less and she'll be happier and
less pressured."

Staying for Now, Planning to Leave
You may be staying for now but keeping your options open for many
reasons:

- Your children are very young and you can't or don't want to man-
  age alone.
- You're financially dependent on the NP/BP.
- You're hoping that you can make enough changes on your own to
  make the relationship more pleasant and tolerable.
- You're still hoping the NP/BP will change.
- Your children are nearly out of high school, and splitting would
  make it hard on everyone.
- You're too depressed and confused to make such a big change as
  leaving.
- You're afraid if you split that the NP/BP will harm the children
  when they're alone with her/him.

If you are . . .
Exploring the possible options of staying or leaving, and/or *not feeling strong enough* to leave, we highly recommend that you find a good

therapist who can help you think through the possibilities, learn the skills you may need, and heal whatever fear and pain you have. Until you really know what you want and decide what is best for you in the long run, it's hard to make a decision and follow through with a plan.

If you are . . .

Trying out changes that you can make to lower the volatility and get along better with your partner, we hope this book is helpful. There are also many books out about understanding the narcissistic and border-line disorders and how to respond more effectively. It can be helpful to try out new behaviors to see what changes may happen. Check out the appendix in the back of this book for a list of helpful books.

If you are . . .

Waiting to see if the NP/BP will follow through with changes he/she has promised to make, it can feel like one step forward and one step back. We suggest that you give yourself a time line and keep accurate track of your interactions during that time. NP/BPs tend to go in cycles of good functioning alternating with volatile, demanding, irrational cycles. So, keep a calendar. Mark the positive days and the negative ones by whatever criteria you choose. Follow through for a month or two and see the real level of positive to negative. It can help you decide what you need or want to do next.

If you are . . .

Parenting children who are very young or about to move out on their own, it can be the soundest choice to stay for a while and prepare to leave when the time works well for you and the children. This is often the hardest choice because you can feel like you're treading water. On the other hand, when you have a goal in mind, your interim choices can be more carefully decided; for example, not signing a new mortgage with your partner, saving money for future needs, finding employment if you haven't been working, and so on.

Whether you plan to stay long term or short term, we recommend that you talk to a lawyer who specializes in family law to find out your legal rights. NP/BPs are very prone to threatening you with taking away your children, leaving you destitute, or controlling all of the family funds. Knowing your rights can help you feel more in control, and help you plan for the contingency of the NP/BP leaving you.

Kindra

Kindra and Tyler have been married for five years and have a son, Aidan, age two. They both have jobs and pretty hectic schedules. "I wouldn't be able to handle being a single parent," Kindra says. "I really love Tyler. I know he has some problems with anger. His temper can get out of hand, but he's only twenty-nine, and I really think he's adjusting to a lot with his job, the marriage, and now Aidan. I'm learning how not to bring up problems when he's stressed, and we're seeing a counselor to help us learn to communicate better. I just want to give this a chance."

Considerations for Leaving

How do you decide if you should stay or leave? Ultimately, that's a very personal decision. It seems to come down to: How are your children being treated by the NP/BP, and how are you being treated?

You may want to leave because the NP/BP is treating one or more of the children badly. Or you may see that one or more of your children are seriously floundering. On the other hand, you may think you can be more protective if you stay so you can watch and counteract the NP/BP's behavior. Or, you may decide that your children will be better off if they're primarily with you and only with the NP/BP part of the time.

Consider, also, your own treatment by the NP/BP. Your marriage is the model for your children of how a love relationship works. Showing your children what you want them to learn about relationships, as well as your emotional well-being, are both important to their continued healthy development. Are you able to stay positive, civil, encouraging, and confident? Or are you becoming worn down, hopeless, depressed, and anxious? How often are you having conflicts with your partner? Are you being demeaned and humiliated in front of the children? How hostile and antagonistic are your interactions with your partner? Do you still love your partner? Do you feel loved?

You need to also think about how much turmoil and uproar a separation or divorce might cause. Will it be worth it to you to not be together? Will you and your children's lives be better? It's also important to consider the fact that whether you stay together or divorce, you and the NP/BP will continue to interact, care for, and make decisions about the children you have together. And over the years you will both go to their weddings and share grandchildren.

Divorce won't end your interactions, but it may create more space in your life to live with more happiness, health, and independence. It allows you and the children to be away from an oppressive atmosphere of hostility and hypervigilance. It can certainly give you space to think, run your home the way you choose, and parent the way you feel is best.

If you are considering divorce, it is essential that you to talk with a lawyer about what that entails and what options you have concerning spousal support, as well as child custody, child support, and parenting time. Divorce from someone with narcissism or borderline issues can be contentious, so learning about your rights and considering the choices you may be facing will be extremely helpful. Many lawyers will give you a short, free consultation to discuss the general rules of your state and to discuss what they can do to help in your situation. Whether you decide to divorce or not, this information is invaluable.

Karyl McBride, in her book, *Will I Ever Be Free of You?*[1] suggests that even very mild or seemingly cooperative NP/BPs can become quite hostile, stubborn, combative, and belligerent during a divorce proceeding, so select a lawyer who is familiar with antagonistic or high-conflict divorces. Give your lawyer specific examples of the NP/BP's behaviors, and ask about their past experience with proceedings involving someone with a personality disorder. Don't expect your lawyer to act as a therapist. Lawyers are trained to be businesslike and to deal with solving problems. They will tend to be matter of fact and will give you information about options. However, they won't be willing to tell you what choices to make.

How do you judge if your relationship is good enough to stay—or bad enough to leave? Here's some information that may be helpful. John Gottman and Robert Levenson[2] have done over twenty years of research with over three thousand couples. They have identified the behaviors between partners in a couple that predict the likelihood of a relationship ending:

- increasing *criticism* of personality or character
- *contempt* expressed in words and body language

- *defensiveness* and not listening
- *stonewalling* by ignoring and refusing to respond to personal concerns

They say that when couples emotionally withdraw and there's an absence of positive feelings during conflict discussions—such as a lack of shared humor, affection, or empathy—there's a high likelihood of a relationship ending. Using these criteria, Gottman and Levenson have been able to predict with 90 percent accuracy whether a marriage relationship will end or not. Unfortunately, their research shows that most couples wait an average of six years after these difficulties appear before seeking help for their problems.

Gottman and Levenson report that in stable relationships there are an average of five positive interactions to each negative. Whereas in unstable relationships, the ratio is .8 negative interactions for every positive—that's almost one negative for every positive. Keeping count of the positive and negative interactions you and your partner have daily can give you a good predictor of where your relationship is going and may help you decide whether you're staying or leaving.

Too often the caretaker partner feels powerless and mystified wait-ing for the NP/BP to decide what will happen in the relationship. Delegating the decisions about your life and future to a partner with such serious disabilities in empathy and emotional understanding just doesn't make sense. If you're staying only because you don't want to be a "failure," consider the environment in which you and your children are living. How successful does it feel?

Making your own decision to stay or to leave is empowering. When you know where YOU stand about the future of your relationship with the NP/BP, you can let go of much of your anger, annoyance, and dis-satisfaction. When you no longer feel *forced* to stay or think you *have* to stay, you'll feel less need to blame the NP/BP for your feelings. When you clearly know that your choice to leave or stay is the best choice, you will have a greater feeling of control and authority over your life. If you're staying, it's with the full knowledge of what you'll need to do both as a partner and a parent. And if you decide to leave, you can create a plan that can work for you and the children both now and in the future.

CHAPTER SEVENTEEN

~

Parenting in the Same Household

A Lot on Your Shoulders

If you're choosing to parent in the same household with a NP/BP partner, you probably think your relationship with your partner is functional enough to keep on working together, at least for the time being. Some NP/BP's can be pretty good parents much of the time. Your partner may be the primary wage earner while you are the primary parent. Or, your partner's emotional dysregulation may be infrequent enough that the benefits of staying connected as a family outweigh the difficulties. We encourage you to pay attention to your own and your children's feelings and continue to monitor and gauge the health and well-being of your family system. It's easy to get hyperfocused on your NP/BP partner and not see the whole picture.

You will probably have a lot of complicated balancing to do, and you're likely to feel pulled between the needs of your children and the demands of the NP/BP. You may often find yourself feeling unsupported and with no clear idea of how to handle all these competing needs. However, knowing you want to create the best possible environment for your family, and having a clear sense of your own values, can help you focus on what's important.

Compassion and Concern

We encourage you to take over most of the parenting duties—especially setting rules, disciplining, and monitoring children's activities. These responsibilities often cause stress for the NP/BP and may create conflicts and arguments. When you see that your partner has a particular parenting activity that is repeatedly upsetting or easily spirals out of control, wait until he/she is emotionally recovered, and calmly bring up the situation when the two of you are alone. Don't criticize your partner's parenting, but approach it with compassion and concern; for example:

- I can see that dealing with Jamie's homework after your hard day is a lot to ask. I'd be happy to help with her homework.
- I'm wondering if making school lunches for all three kids is really wearing you down. I think they're old enough to make their own lunches. Let me get them organized to do that and take that off your shoulders.
- You sounded pretty upset the other night trying to get Charlie to turn off the TV and go to bed. I'm sorry that he's so stubborn. Let me give it a try tonight. You go ahead with your project in the garage, and I'll see what I can do.

These examples include statements of facts, an empathetic comment toward your partner, and an offer of help. Be careful to avoid demands, criticism, or any implication of incompetence.

Don't Argue; Separate Instead

Although episodes where the NP/BP is unsympathetic and argumentative with the children may make you frustrated and angry, quarreling with your partner will not help the situation. You cannot win an argument with a narcissist or borderline person. Keep your eye on the goal of making your home environment peaceful and conducive for health and well-being. Skillfully move your partner-parent and the children apart in pleasant, nonattacking ways.

This requires you to step in to solve problems without condemning anyone, and without siding with either your partner or your child. Your job is more of a referee, therapist, and problem solver. Separate the parties, and then listen to each one's grievances separately. Empathizing privately with each party will avoid inflaming the other. Your comments need to be supportive, but you don't have to agree with the person. Mostly you need to say things that are empathetic, helpful, and also motivating enough to get cooperation.

For your kids:

- I can help you with your homework. Then you can watch TV from 8 to 9.
- Your dad is pretty upset right now that you're an hour late past curfew. You didn't get grounded this time, but what can we do to fix that next time?
- Arguing with your mom doesn't work. Leave it for now and check in with her tomorrow. She often changes her mind.
- What your dad said really hurt your feelings. I want you to know I think you're really trying hard.

For your partner:

- I get why you're upset and yelled at the children. I need you to know I'm here to help. Let me know when the kids are getting to you, and I can step in so you don't have to handle things alone.
- I get the feeling you think I'm not helping enough. I want you to know I'm here to support you.
- It sounds like you think Henry did something wrong. What exactly upset you? (Listen) I understand.

Time Outs

It can be emotionally challenging for you to continually empathize when your own feelings may have been triggered and you're also angry and overwhelmed. Separating your partner-parent and the children is a way to create time outs for them. However, you need to give yourself the leniency of time outs as well.

When you're upset, take yourself out of the situation and do something that helps you calm down and be more able to think rationally again. Margalis: My favorite is taking a brisk walk. It really clears my head. Make a list of things that work for you—whether it's quiet time, vigorous exercise, talking with a friend or therapist, journaling, doing a hobby you enjoy, or whatever. When you have so much required of you, you need a lot of self-compassion and good self-care.

When you're rested and level-headed again, you can look at the situation more effectively and apply the problem-solving techniques from chapter 12. Then you can be more effective with both your partner and your children. Few problems have to be solved immediately—despite everyone around you thinking that they do. If you're angry and confused, offer an immediate comment of compassion and concern, then take a breather to consider what could be more workable in the long-run.

Create a Parenting Agreement

Most couples probably don't identify explicit expectations about how they will parent. However, since you and your partner may often find yourselves at odds about parenting behaviors, especially in heated moments, it's really an advantage to discuss. Talking about HOW you want to parent ahead of time can help you both during the more hectic and upsetting moments with children that can pop up with little notice. Things you might want to talk about include:

- Do you believe that children are naturally good or naturally misbehaving?
- What are your hopes and dreams for each of your children?
- Who is the stricter parent? Who is more lenient? Explain why.
- Do you see children as a pleasure? Or more as work?
- How do you feel about shouting, yelling, and screaming to get children's attention?
- Are you against spanking children? Or is that OK?
- Do you expect your children to obey whatever you say? Or do you prefer to talk things out with your children?

It's likely that there are other topics you might talk through as well, but this gives you an idea of some possibilities. It's important to do this in a quiet and calm way. Acknowledge your differences without arguing or trying to convince the other person to change his/her mind. Write down the comments and expectations you come up with, noting where you agree and where you differ. Keep these in a notebook and refer back to them in future discussions.

Some couples find it positive and helpful to write up a family statement of the values and beliefs they agree on. For example:

> We believe that parents should be in charge of the family. We expect our children to obey, be polite, and respect others. It is our job to provide food, shelter, support, teaching, and love to our children. When we don't agree, we believe in polite discussion without hitting, screaming, or rudeness. It's the parents' job to come up with solutions that work.
>
> We believe in love, respect, and honoring the individuality of each person in the family. Our goal is to provide an atmosphere of kindness, consideration, and caring. We are willing to listen to each other. We believe in compromise and working to understand each other when there are disagreements. Our job as parents is to nurture, teach by example, and protect the well-being of each person in the family.

Of course, you'll come up with a family statement that fits your combined values. When you have a working agreement, you can refer back to it in difficult times to get back on track with less argument or criticism. You can say, "We both want the best for our children. I can see you're really angry right now. We've agreed to listen and talk calmly. Is there anything I can do to help resolve this situation with you?" Showing compassion, reminding each other of your goals and values, and offering support can go a long way to avoiding a lot of meltdowns in the parents and in the children.

Family Rules

Setting rules for the whole family can be a challenge. If you've found this process has triggered a lot of chaos, anger, or arguments in the past, here are some suggestions. First of all, everyone above the age of four or five needs to have some input into the rules. However, this doesn't mean democratic rule. Parents ultimately need to be in charge, but children are more cooperative when they have a voice in the process.

One way to get started is to post two lists—one for the parents to write down suggested rules, and one for the children's ideas about the rules. As therapists, we've found that asking children what the rules should be can be very enlightening. They usually have good ideas about rules, and their rules are often more demanding and harsh than you might expect. After a few days, set up a time to talk about *all* the rules from the two lists. Discuss the pros and cons of each one. Children and parents get to say what they like and don't like. You'll probably start to see some common agreement about many of the rules. Write those down and post them.

Take the ones you can't all agree on and discuss these at a later time with your partner. Try to come up with a list you can both live with. Then share those with the children, telling them your reasons. If you're open to more discussion, encourage feedback from the children. Eventually you want a list of all the basic rules that can be signed by everyone and posted.

Why do we suggest that you post the rules? Keeping the rules in sight encourages more cooperation from the children—as well as from your partner. Instead of criticizing each other, you can simply refer to the agreed-upon rules. Although this won't always work, it will work a great deal of the time. And it tends to diminish whining and arguments. It's also a good idea to revisit the rules every few months to see if changes are needed. Follow the same procedure of collecting suggestions and then discussing.

Enhance Positive Interactions with Your Partner

Pay attention to the positive traits and interests of your partner. Notice what she/he enjoys doing with the children and encourage these interactions. You can also do a lot to help set up these positive experiences.

- Raleigh noticed that although his wife liked doing fun things with their son, she had trouble thinking of things to do, so, with her agreement, he would set up events, buy the tickets, and send them off to the aquarium, movies, and baseball games together.

- Sandie would come home from work exhausted and need a little quiet time to herself. She knew Danny liked taking the children to the park, so she'd encourage them all to go to the park while she cooked dinner in the quiet kitchen.

When you and your partner regularly do things together that the other likes, it can make some room for you to do things alone or with your friends without your partner. Later when your partner complains that you never pay attention, you can remind him/her of the good times you just had together.

Assertive Communication

Clear Statements, Answers, and Questions

You need to be clear and assertive in your communication with an NP/BP partner. Don't assume she/he will get your message unless you make a clear statement about what you want to convey. Instead of saying, "That sounds nice," say "Yes, I'd like to do that." Instead of assuming your partner will automatically take over doing the dishes, cleaning, or caring for the children in your absence, ask him/her to be there. "I'm going to my meeting at 5. There's food in the oven. Would you please see that the children get fed?" You may think these daily tasks are obvious, but they often aren't on the NP/BP's radar if they aren't part of a normal pattern.

How to Say NO

Saying "No" can be tricky with an NP/BP partner. It can trigger their defensiveness and anger. Try to avoid the actual word *No*, and include an offer or incentive.

- That won't work for me tonight, however, I'd be free on Wednesday.
- I can see you'd like to visit your mom this weekend. I'm overwhelmed with a work project. It's OK with me if you go yourself or take the kids with you.
- I'd prefer Chinese food tonight. I'm happy to drive.

Don't Expect Agreement

Be aware of which of your needs, wants, and boundaries are most important to you. Figure out how to get these fulfilled as often as possible without the help of the NP/BP. However, stand firm on the things that are seriously important to you. Be diplomatic and firmly stubborn about those. Don't ask for permission; instead, state what you will do, don't engage in discussion, but consider the needs of your partner. You'll have the most success with things that you can control.

- Dinner is at 5. If you're not here, I'll leave you a plate in the fridge.
- My exercise class is on Mondays and Wednesdays. Can you be home to watch the children? (If yes) Great. Thank you. I appreciate your help. (If not) I'll get the sitter to come in.
- I really like it when the house is clean. We don't seem to have enough time to get everything done, so I've hired a house cleaner to come in on Fridays. It will be a big help to us both.
- My dad will be in town next week. I haven't seen him much lately. He and I will be meeting for dinner on Tuesday.

Stay Connected to Others

Don't Isolate

People with NP/BP are often very jealous of your time and attention. They also want to keep their more negative behaviors hidden from others. So, they may try to isolate you from family, friends, and outside activities. They may encourage or even demand that you not talk to certain people, not talk about particular topics, keep secrets, or even lie on their behalf. You need to decide for yourself which of these commands you will acquiesce to. It is essential to your mental health and well-being that you stay connected to family and friends. Even if you have to keep these connections private, it will be important to not become isolated.

The NP/BP may encourage you to quit working, to homeschool the children, or see only certain people of their choosing. These are all ways to move you into a powerless position in the relationship. This isolation can negatively impact your children's socialization skills, understanding of reality, and emotional development. You may think that giving in will make it easier to get along with the NP/BP, but the negative impacts on you and the children can be severe. These are issues worth challenging and being stubborn about.

Stay Grounded and Rational

The NP/BP lives in a delusional world in which their needs and wants are the most important. They work hard to control the actions and even thoughts of their family members to conform to their delusions. Without outside connections, you can get drawn into their fantasies and misbeliefs—many of which are very negative about you—and you can end up thinking you're crazy and become seriously depressed, anxious, or unable to think clearly. Keep yourself tuned into reality by checking in with others about how you feel, who you are, and how they see you.

Don't try to talk your NP/BP partner into seeing things more rationally when he/she is caught up in a delusion about you or the world, because he/she will not be able to access their rational mind at that time. Walk away, and don't participate in discussions that aren't based in reality. If you get pulled into arguing about what's good/bad, right/wrong, real/false, you can quickly lose your perspective and your cool. Stay calm and exit as quickly as possible. These discussions only exacerbate the NP/BP's anger and fantastic imaginings.

Community Connections Are Essential for You

You will need as much community support as possible. You can be deceived by the NP/BP into thinking that if you give in to his/her demands to isolate that it will make things at home less contentious and distressing, but it will not. Keeping secrets, pretending all is well, and putting on a false persona will only make you and your children more vulnerable to the NP/BP's unreasonable demands and oppressive control.

You need to have at least two or three friends or family members who know about and understand your home situation. They need to be mentally healthy, compassionate, and clear headed. We strongly suggest that you also have a therapist or counselor who is knowledgeable about your partner's mental state, and who can offer a listening ear as well as practical suggestions. In addition, you need some kind of social life apart from your partner. This is most easily accomplished by joining with other parents where your children go to school, when they play in sports, and attend family-oriented social activities. Volunteer to help with projects, outings, and even help out in your child's classroom. It's a great way to show your children that you are there for them, and it will provide you with a continuing realistic baseline of how other parents are caring for and raising their children.

Connections for Your Children

Help your children find things they love to do—sports, art, music, school clubs, and others. Encourage them to participate, and make time to help them get to meetings, practices, and events. Don't assume that your partner will participate in making these things happen. You might find it difficult to host other children or families in your home for sleepovers, dinners, or social activities because you can't predict your partner's reactions. Instead, join other families in carpools, picnics in the park, and trips to sports or other events. If your partner doesn't want to take part, go without him/her. You might face some pouting, silence, or caustic remarks from the NP/BP, but it can be worth it to connect with others and see the delight your children experience.

Enjoy Your Children

Many people who have a NP/BP partner find that they get great satisfaction from focusing their energy and attention on enjoying their role as parent, even when the relationship with their partner doesn't meet their full expectations. Knowing that you are doing your best to encourage and support your children's development into the healthy adults they can be, and enjoying their childhood with them, can be greatly fulfilling. Being a good parent can give you hours of joy and satisfaction. You don't have to be perfect, and your children don't have to be perfect for you to know you have a good connection and you're responsive, validating, and caring. And when your children know you really care, they can be amazingly accepting of your mistakes or difficulties. Your relationship with your children is lifelong. It's worth all the investment you can put into it, and the rewards you receive as a connected, involved parent can balance out some of the deficiencies in your relationship with your partner.

~

CHAPTER EIGHTEEN

Parenting after Divorce

Parenting after divorce, or the end of a significant relationship, from a NP/BP partner brings its own challenges. You may hope that a divorce means you no longer have to deal with the drama and chaos that come with living in a Narcissistic Family System. Once you are living in separate homes, you will certainly have more control over life for you and your children. You will be better able to manage, and often avoid, the uproar that comes from the NP/BP parent. But as long as you have children together and share parenting time and parental responsibilities, you will remain connected and have to at least minimally interact. Divorce doesn't end a family; it simply changes the form of it.

The information we have presented in the preceding chapters applies whether you are living together or are separated. This chapter will focus on additional actions specific to parenting after separation or divorce that will help you help your children.

Coparenting Won't Work

For the majority of divorced parents, cooperative parenting is a viable option that runs along a continuum ranging from a great deal of communication between parents to more limited communication and interaction. You may receive advice from well-meaning friends and family to try to get along with your ex. Coparenting sounds like such a reasonable idea, and you will find a great deal of information about it in books, magazine articles, and online. The term *coparenting* is a shortened version of the phrase *cooperative parenting*. Key to effective coparenting is a willingness and ability to share information, cooperate with parenting issues, and protect children from adult conflict. Coparenting requires both parents to be willing to talk with each other, negotiate differences of opinion at times, and be open to compromise when it comes to what's best for their children. This is highly unlikely to occur with a NP/BP parent. If you try to coparent, you will very likely find it to be a disappointing and frustrating experience, where you, and by extension your children, end up feeling used, devalued, and out of control.

Parallel Parenting

Parallel parenting is much more effective and successful with divorced families marked by ongoing conflict, and it is our recommendation for separated and/or divorced parents dealing with a NP/BP parenting partner. In parallel parenting, there is no expectation of regular communication between parents. Each home is separate and somewhat autonomous. Both parents remain actively involved with their children, but not with each other. Think of two streets running side by side with very few locations where they intersect. Parallel parenting is marked by the following attributes:

- Parents communicate about emergencies, but not day-to-day issues.
- Parents do not communicate face to face; instead, they use online communication programs and/or structured email and text messaging.
- The parent given decision-making authority by the court communicates decisions with the other parent. There is no joint discussion.
- Homes are separate, with each parent dealing with day-to-day issues about the children when they are in that household. Accept the fact that there may be different rules in each home.

- Cultures in each home may be quite different, and may cause some distress to children moving between homes.
- The parenting plan is followed exactly with no requests for adjustments or change.
- Parents may require an external authority like a therapist, mediator, or parenting coordinator/arbitrator to help with conflict or lack of agreement.
- Each parent is responsible for his/her relationship with the children. There is no expectation that the other parent will offer help or support.

Think of parallel parenting as your foundation for interacting with the other parent. It probably won't work all of the time, because NP/BP partners thrive on stirring things up and getting their way. But parallel parenting will help you provide healthy boundaries and thereby offer some peace of mind as you work your way through parenting after divorce. Here are some tips to help you get started on the parallel parenting path:

1. Never involve yourself in the other parent's life and actions. That means no quizzing the kids about who's at the other parent's house. No cyber stalking or driving past their house. It means not involving friends or family to get information. It truly means letting go of caring. Pick your battles carefully, and step in only when it is a significant matter for your child. For example, you must intervene with things that you simply cannot ignore, like physical safety, abuse, medical concerns, and/or mental health issues.
2. Adopt a businesslike approach when dealing with the other parent. Don't reveal personal information. Don't send chatty emails. Keep agreements exactly. Keep interactions brief and focused on the outcome. Have no expectations that the other parent will care about you and your needs and feelings. Resist the urge to make changes or accommodations for the NP/BP with the hope he/she will reciprocate. This is no longer a give-and-take relationship.

3. Maintain a courteous demeanor, and don't react to criticism, belittling, and name-calling. Likewise, don't initiate these behaviors.

4. Keep your focus on the present task at hand, even when the other parent will try to distract you or manipulate you to their advantage. Two phrases that work well are "nevertheless" and "that may be." Here's an example of how to use them: your six-year-old daughter has a soccer match and has left her only team jersey at the other parent's house. You've just realized the jersey is missing and the match is in an hour. She is upset and crying, worried that she won't be allowed to play. Reluctantly, you send a text asking about the jersey, and the other parent replies that yes, it is at her house. She goes on to tell you what a lousy parent you are for not being more on top of this, completely ignoring the fact that she is the one that didn't send it with your daughter. "This is just like you," she texts back. "You never did a thing around the house to help me. And I see you haven't changed a bit." You are at a choice point here. You can try to defend yourself, which won't work. Or you can attack her, which also won't work. Instead, you don't take the bait that she is dangling before you. "That may be," you reply. "But right now, I need Alicia's jersey. If you put it in a bag and leave it on the doorstep, I can pick it up on the way to the soccer field."

5. Let go of past interactions and disappointments.

6. Approach every interaction by asking yourself this question: "How will this affect our child?" Then act accordingly.

7. Do your best to minimize conflict, especially if your children are present.

8. Keep a written record of all agreements, discussions, and changes.

9. Rely on the help of a neutral third party when you need to work something out.

10. Follow your parenting plan exactly, and do not ask for changes.

We are well aware that the ten suggestions on this list may sound simple and easy to do, but in fact they are not. Each one of these ten requires an enormous amount of self-discipline and emotional energy from you, and at times you will feel like giving up. But keep at it. Like learning any new skill, the more you practice nonengagement and holding firm boundaries, the easier it will become. Never lose sight of the fact that you are doing this for your children.

Make Your Home a Sanctuary

Within your household, there are things you can do that will greatly help your children feel emotionally and physically safe. Create an environment of peace and order for yourself and your children. Establish predictable routines around meals, bedtime, chores, and expectations. Help your children know details of parenting plans, like when they will be at each home. With young children, having a calendar with stickers for mom's house and dad's house will help them know what to expect. It also helps to talk in terms of "sleeps" rather than days. For example, "You'll sleep at Daddy's for three nights, and then you'll come back here." This kind of detail helps children feel in control of events and their lives. Older children may not need stickers on a calendar, but they will likely need reminding about the plans. Develop systems for moving your children's belongings between homes. If possible, have duplicate items for basic clothing and personal care needs. Don't punish your children when they leave something at the other parent's house. Transitioning between homes is rather like international travel, and it can be overwhelming and exhausting. Anything you can do to ease the process will reduce stress for your children.

Stay in Your Role as the Adult

Protect your children from conflict that you may have with the other parent. It is simply not their business, and more importantly, it is damaging to them. Multiple studies over time have shown that parental conflict is the biggest predictor of poor outcome for children. Keeping children out of your conflict is one of the greatest gifts you will ever give them. Don't criticize or badmouth the other parent or put your children in the position of having to take sides.

Tempting as it might be, never use your children as a sounding board for your feelings. Even when they ask you, use good judgment about what you share. "I'm not willing to have that conversation with you right now," sets a healthy boundary and protects your children. Find appropriate outlets for your feelings so that you don't rely on your children to take care of you. Make use of friends, family, support groups, and therapy to work through your feelings.

While children may complain about household rules, the boundaries that you set, and consequences for behaviors, they provide important emotional safety that children may not receive when at the other parent's house.

Expect Uproar

Parenting with a NP/BP partner isn't going to be easy. They don't follow rules because they believe they are above them. They will break agreements. They will try to make you out to be the "bad guy" and blame you for anything and everything. You must become a master at Plan B. And while it may not feel fair, it is quite simply how it is. Be prepared for the other parent to change plans at the last minute. Be the source of consistency and predictability for your children. Always be ready to take care of your children when the other parent can't or won't. It may feel as if you are supporting irresponsible behavior. What you are really doing is providing a safety net for your precious children. Never forget that.

Limitations and Benefits

As with most everything in life, there are pros and cons to consider when parenting after divorce with a NP/BP parenting partner. We've already discussed some of the limitations, but here are a few more to consider.

- Your children's lives will be more complicated. Moving between households is at best challenging. Children don't get to do everything they want. They are constantly saying goodbye to one parent, one home, one neighborhood. They may not be able to participate in as many activities with friends. They may miss out on family events when with the other parent. They may have to navigate living in distinctly different homes with different rules and expectations.

- Working out vacations, holidays, and other celebrations can be difficult. It often becomes more about the adults than the children, and your kids will resent that.
- Children in divorced families often face disappointment when parents change plans, when a parent doesn't show up, or when parents make promises they don't keep.
- When children are living in two different homes, they are likely to be exposed to things you don't like. When your children are with the other parent, you have very little control, especially when you aren't able to share information. There are frequently differences in values, lifestyle choices, religion, food, house rules, and friends.

There are also benefits for your children. In tough times, it helps to remember these.

- The home you provide for your children is emotionally safe. It is a sanctuary for them—a place to relax, to learn and grow in developmentally appropriate ways, and a place to have fun. Within your household you create a healthy, rational, chaos-free, and trauma-free environment.
- Your children learn to handle life's challenges with coping skills and resilience. This will serve them well as they become adults.
- In your home, your children can feel free to invite their friends over, free of the worry and embarrassment about what the NP/BP parent might say or do.
- Because of the routine and predictability you have created, your children can relax and know what to expect. This leaves them free to grow and develop in age-appropriate ways. This structure allows them to have a childhood.

Gather Your Team

It is going to be important for you to create a team to help you as you parent your children with a NP/BP parent. You don't have to do this by yourself. Think of the often-quoted African proverb that states, "It takes a village to raise a child." This has resonated with so many people because it rings true. Parenting alone is hard. Parenting with support is much easier. So, who will you place on your team?

- As you work through your divorce, you will want a *good attorney*. Ask questions and interview until you find someone you trust. Make sure they have a working understanding of the unique issues you face with a NP/BP partner. You will want an attorney who will help you craft a clear and workable parenting plan that clearly covers the issues that will arise. You want to leave as little to chance as possible.
- A *parenting coordinator* (PC) with arbitration ability. There are going to be issues that you simply cannot resolve with the other parent. If you have agreed to use a PC to resolve disputes, it will help considerably. Get this person in place at the beginning so that when the first issue arises, you have a means to address it.
- Find a *support group and/or your own personal therapist*. This will quite honestly be one of the best things you do for yourself. Throughout this book, we have stated what a huge job you have ahead of you as you try to parent with a NP/BP partner. Getting support is key to helping you be able to do this. Again, look for professionals with knowledge and experience with narcissistic family systems.
- Keep an eye on your children and get them into therapy if needed. Navigating this particular family system isn't easy, and it is very likely that your children will benefit from having someone to help them. Talking with a knowledgeable adult who they know isn't on either side is often a relief and immensely helpful.
- Line up *good childcare*. There will be times when you need a babysitter. It doesn't make you a bad parent. It will offer you great peace of mind to know ahead of time who you can call on when you need help. It could be a friend, family member, or someone else. Keep a list of names and numbers at the ready. As much as possible, try to have the same childcare person. Make that person part of your team.

- Keep your *friends* in the loop. This is not the time to abandon your friends. You are going to need all the support you can find.
- If you have a good relationship with *your family*, rely on them to provide support and continuity. The larger supportive community you and your children have, the better.

Parenting after divorce is complicated in the best of circumstances. With a NP/BP partner it is even more complicated. The process of parallel parenting provides a format that will help you. When you don't expect cooperation from the other parent, you are less likely to be disappointed, frustrated, or blind-sided. Maintaining healthy boundaries, not taking the bait the other parent is sure to repeatedly place in your path, and always putting your children's needs at the forefront of your actions will serve you well. While this isn't gong to be easy, it is something you can do. Enlist others to help and support you. Stay in your role as the adult. Make your home a safe place for your children and for you.

CHAPTER NINETEEN

~

Being a Good Enough Parent

From Margalis

What I want to leave you with is that children are naturally resilient. They have their own awareness about what is going on in the family. Everything they see and hear they use to make their best guess about how to respond. Most children are very aware and responsive to the emotional environment, but they often lack the information and experience to interpret the whole picture or know what to expect will happen. They have a natural optimism that hasn't been jaded by years of hurt and disappointment, and even though they may seem distraught over not going to the zoo or missing a birthday party, they bounce back as soon as some new possibility appears.

It's also important to remember that your children have an entirely different relationship to their other parent than you have. Behaviors of the NP/BP that are deeply hurtful to you may not matter or even be understood by your children. In addition, they typically receive a lot of positive interactions with their other parent as well. So, don't assume that you always know what they're feeling or, even, that they're feeling the same things you are. That's why keeping an open dialogue with your children can be of such great benefit. You can get real-time assessments about how they're doing and be better able to support them.

Mostly what your children need from you is to *see* who they are as individuals, to appreciate, enjoy, and love who they are, to value their unique characteristics and talents, and to be kind and considerate in helping them grapple with the issues and situations that they don't know how to handle or aren't yet proficient in.

Each child will respond to his/her life situation differently. Most children are able to thrive no matter what their family circumstances happen to be—unless, of course, if there is extreme abuse, poverty, or rejection.

W. Thomas Boyce, MD says most children are like dandelions and can grow and thrive almost anywhere.[1] However, a few children, about 20 percent, are more like orchids and need special care and attention. Because the susceptibility of borderline and narcissism characteristics often flow through families, you may see some of those traits or vulnerabilities in your children. Teaching your children to soothe their upset feelings, giving them quiet spaces to calm themselves, and helping them learn that they can overcome their anger and hurt feelings can be tremendously helpful. Learned early, these self-regulating behaviors can make a huge difference in their ability to cope throughout their lives.

Setting firm boundaries with kindness and consideration rather than with anger or extreme punishments will create a safe haven. Help your children talk through their mistakes and misjudgments rather than using banishment, hostility, or negative comments. Instead, calmly engage them in a questioning dialogue, such as:

- How did this happen?
- What do you think you could do about this?
- Why did you decide to do this?
- What would you do next time?
- What do you think I should do about this?
- If that doesn't work, how will you handle it?

When you approach your children as amazing, interesting, developing human beings and get to know them, your parenting approach moves from being the controller and enforcer to being more like a scientist who is getting to know, understand, and appreciate your children's rare and unique culture and view of the world.

Julie Lythcott-Haims in her book *How to Raise an Adult* suggests that helping your children learn to take care of themselves and function well in the adult world is the real goal of parenting.[2] Setting clear boundaries and expectations while also being responsive to your children's needs works the best. However, specific parenting styles aren't as important as teaching your children to:

- value themselves and at the same time appreciate and value others.
- be able to work with joy and passion.
- be helpful to others.
- problem solve and figure things out for themselves.
- think for themselves.
- accept their own imperfections.
- bounce back from difficulties.

As an easy shorthand reminder for good enough parenting, I suggest remembering the adage Keep Calm and Carry On.[3] The acronym CALM, which stands for *curiosity, acceptance, loving compassion,* and *motivation,* can be a quick prompt to summarize your job as a positive parent.

Curiosity
Children learn to be curious when they feel safe to explore and don't have to be perfect.

- Give your children plenty of time for unstructured experimenting—lots of free play, planting a garden, learning their neighborhood, experimenting with building projects, cooking experiments, art endeavors, and more.
- Help them meet lots of people, get to know the neighbors, interact on their own with other children's parents, and participate in community activities.
- Give them room to experiment, make mistakes, and learn from them, try out new ways to do things, have time to daydream, and ask millions of questions.
- Provide space for them to invent, rearrange, create, and make messes.

Don't worry too much about how other people think you should be raising your children. Think about what makes life interesting to your own unique children.

Acceptance

Your acceptance of each of your children with their own set of abilities, difficulties, joys, and fears sets them on the path to feeling safe, loved, and valued. Whether they're outgoing or shy, intellectually inclined or hands-on experimenters, athletic or artistic, your acceptance and support of who they are at the moment and in all the many versions of themselves as they develop is an important key to raising resilient kids.

Loving Compassion

Children who feel loved and cared for and are given limits and boundaries turn out to have higher academic achievement, less depression, and fewer problems with aggression and disobedience. Let your children know that you love them dearly, *and* you expect them to follow the rules, help out with chores, take care of themselves and their belongings, and take responsibility for their behavior. This gives them a sense of security and trust.

Motivation

Remember that humans feel more motivated when they know that their actions matter and that they can have an impact on what happens to them. When you encourage your children to participate in decisions, when you ask about their feelings and perspectives, and when you consider their views and interests, your children will be happier and more motivated to follow through with their responsibilities and agreements.

Good Enough

None of us knows what the world will be like in twenty, thirty, or forty years from now. Those are the years your children will be running things and creating their own families. Try to keep that bigger picture in mind. Are the lessons you're teaching your children now going to be helpful to them then? Will the things you're worried about for your children right now be really important when they're adults?

But mostly, ask yourself, "Although I'm not a perfect parent, am I a good enough parent?" No one is or can be a perfect parent, and it's impossible to control or manufacture the perfect life for your children. The challenge is to combine your understanding and skills and the natural personality traits and individuality of your children, and combine those with the advantages and challenges of your family situation, in a way that you can nurture and support your children. Help them face their challenges and together create solutions that work for them.

Incidental failures along the way are simply bumps in the road. They don't define your identity or your children's future. You and your children have many years beyond this difficult time and family situation. Your care for them now is the foundation of their ability to be strong and independent and loving. So, remember CALM and do your best. You won't always hit the perfect balance, and they won't always respond ideally, but if you keep trying, loving, and working at it, it will be enough.

From Jean

I want to leave you with a large dose of self-compassion. In the best of circumstances, parenting comes with multiple challenges. The truth is, in every family there are going to be hard days. You love your children, and yet there are times when you want to throw your hands in the air and simply give up. This feeling is perfectly normal. Yes, you live in a family system with the additional challenge of parenting with a NP/BP partner. It's easy to blame yourself for falling in love with a narcissist, for choosing to have children together, for staying in the relationship, for leaving, or for any number of other things. There is usually plenty of blame to go around, seasoned with an equal portion of guilt. These feelings aren't helpful to you or your children. In the wise words of my hairdresser, who has probably listened to more life stories than I have in my entire career as a marriage and family therapist, "Girlfriend, you have to let that stuff go."

In her book *Bouncing Back*, author and marriage and family therapist Linda Graham[4] offers five steps to think about when coming to acceptance about something we've done or experienced about which we aren't very happy. The steps are:

1. Here's what happened
2. And what I did to get through it
3. These were the consequences—tempered through a lens of self-compassion
4. I learned this—how this contributes to changing how I think about it and myself
5. Here's how I can move forward

Important in this process is nurturing your self-compassion. Rather than continue beating yourself up over something that's happened, work through these steps to arrive at the last step—the one that helps you accept yourself and move on. Parents aren't perfect. We make mistakes. We do or say things we'd love to reel back as soon as they've happened. Sometimes we totally blow it. When that happens, use these steps to regain your balance and move forward. And let go of the rest.

As you deal with the issues specific to your family, you'll find an avalanche of information and will probably receive more advice than you ever thought possible. You'll hear stories about how your children are doomed and there is nothing you can do to help them. Don't believe it. This simply isn't true, and it's why we wrote this book. We want you to have the support and information necessary to help your children build the resilience they need to thrive, in spite of living in a narcissistic family system. Give yourself a break. Be kind. And remember that continuing to improve your good, basic parenting skills will get you through many, if not most, of the challenges you face.

At the foundation is a parenting style called *authoritative parenting*, first described in the 1960s by psychologist Diana Baumrind and later expanded by numerous others.[5] Authoritative parenting is marked by warm and responsive interactions with children, clear expectations with fair and consistent discipline, and a high value for child independence. Research has repeatedly shown that children raised with authoritative parenting tend to be happy, capable, and successful. When you employ this high-touch, high-expectation style of parenting, it is as if you are surrounding your children with a protective shield.

Safety and trust are at the basis of resilience and healthy brain development. As you nurture resilience in yourself and your children, you create an atmosphere of competence to counteract the stress, disappointments, and trauma of daily life. Think of yourself as the safety officer in your family, as the trust broker for your children. Parenting is never one single act. Like an artist creating a complex painting, we lay down one important layer at a time. It is the accumulation of each small, day-to-day action that directly influences our children's healthy brains and their ability to handle whatever life throws at them. Each time you help your child work through a problem with kindness and compassion, you are helping their brains develop. Each time you provide a refuge of safety, predictability, and trust, you are building healthy brains. Each time you model your own resilience in the face of a difficult or traumatic situation, you are helping your children build their resilience. Neuroscience shows us that our amazing brains develop best through interaction with other brains. For a child, in the early years of her life, that "other brain" is yours. Think of the ramifications of that statement. It truly drives home the importance of parents nurturing their own resilience and well-being.

Let's look at how this might play out in a day-to-day situation. The after-school day care teacher calls you because no one has come to pick up your third-grader and it's closing time. You are instantly angry because this was your husband's responsibility today. You had a late meeting at work and knew you couldn't be finished in time. You excuse yourself from the meeting and make your way to the school, mumbling and cursing all the way. When you arrive, you barely talk to your daughter. You apologize to the teacher for being late, and hustle your daughter to the car. She immediately picks up on your mood and thinks it is her fault—that she is the cause of your anger. On the drive home you keep trying to reach your husband, leaving angry messages each time he doesn't answer. Then you take a call from a friend and rant about the situation and how you can't count on your husband. "He's too involved with himself to ever be any help to me. He doesn't even care about our kids." By the time you arrive home, your daughter is crying. Your anger has contaminated her, and she is in distress. There is no safety and no refuge for her.

So, let's improve this for both of you. You get the call about your husband not picking up your daughter. Your first reaction is still anger. You take a few deep breaths to calm your nervous system, excuse yourself from the meeting, and make your way to the school. You engage curiosity, wondering what happened to detain him. On the way you continue deep breathing and remind yourself that you've got this. "I can handle this," you tell yourself. At the school you hug your daughter, help her gather her things, and buckle her into her seatbelt. In the car on the way home you play your daughter's favorite music, something you know is familiar and calming for her. Once home you take a few quiet minutes together, sitting beside her with your arm around her. "It must have been kind of scary when you thought you'd been left at school," you gently say. You stroke her hair and hold her close because you know that touch is calming, as you listen to her. "I think it was just a mix up," you reply. "I'm sorry we scared you." Your calm demeanor and reassuring tone help to settle her jangled nervous system. You have provided safety and a sense of trust and refuge. And your daughter has learned a valuable lesson in resilience. When your husband comes home, you wait until your daughter is in bed and well asleep before you talk about what happened, protecting her from any discord that may arise.

Resilience is about choices and learning to respond from a place of balance. Each of us has the power within us to choose how we respond. It just takes a bit of practice. Because of something called neuroplasticity, the brain is capable of learning resilience at any age. Linda Graham[6] states, "Resilience is teachable, learnable, and recoverable." This is some of the most comforting, reassuring research I've come across in my work as a therapist. We humans are always capable of growth and change. I can do it, and so can you. A favorite quote of mine from the author and businessman W. Clement Stone is this, "Little hinges swing big doors."[7] We build resilience in ourselves and in our children one small act at a time, over and over.

As you counter the negativity that comes from the other parent, remember the phrase *little and often*. Be the little hinge that swings the big door of your child's healthy brain and developing resilience. You've got this!

~

CHAPTER TWENTY

Final Words

We each want to share a case story of a family in which a child is successfully raised by a borderline or narcissistic parent and a care-taker parent, so you can have a personal view into the dynamics and complexities of this situation. As you know, your family circumstances aren't ideal, but they also aren't necessarily disastrous. We hope these examples give you concrete information about the possibilities.

My Story: Margalis

I am often asked how I got interested in the field of personality disorders. When I was in graduate school, I heard about Borderline Personality Disorder for the first time, and the more I read, the more I realized that I had a vivid understanding of the issues and symptoms. My mother met the criteria for the disorder. For each symptom, I had a significant childhood memory or story about her behavior. The only criteria she never met was that of suicidality.

It the 1970s there was no information about or for family members and how they were affected, no idea about why BPD occurred, and no information on what to do about the disorder. I was told that my grandmother took my mother to the Menninger Clinic in Topeka, Kansas, for help. My grandmother was told in the second session that she had caused my mother's difficult behaviors. That was the last time they went in. We have learned so much since then, and in just the last ten years brain science has increased our understanding tremendously. Family environments have a powerful impact, but so does inherited brain dysfunction.

How Did Being Raised by a Borderline Mother Affect Me?

I was actually raised by three parents—my mother, father, and grandmother. The reason I knew my grandmother didn't *cause* my mother's problems was that she was so kind, loving, and gentle with me and my two younger sisters. She lived next door, and I probably spent 40 percent of my time at her house with the chickens, the garden, playing, and being cared for. Many of the things I needed to learn about the world, relationships, and being me I got from her.

My father was kind, gentle, funny, and took us on vacations to visit his brothers and sisters in California. He taught my sisters and me to ride bikes and mow the grass, built us a swing set, helped us with school projects, and dutifully came to our dance performances.

My mother was a talented seamstress and knitter—two things I enjoy doing as well. She made great desserts, and kept the house tidy. She also had frequent emotional meltdowns that included screaming, hitting, and throwing things, alternating with migraine headaches that went on for days. She had these hysterics almost always when my dad was at work, and, somehow, we learned we were never to tell him. Generally, she was distant, rarely engaged in conversation, and I only remember sitting on her lap once. Her hugs felt like my energy was being drained. However, for years she attended a lady's church group in which she was well liked and friendly. She was an enigma to me, and I kept searching for the magical way I could get her attention and her caring. In order to escape the turmoil, I spent hours reading and living in a fantasy world.

Things I Didn't Learn or Know Very Well

I am the oldest of three girls, so I didn't have an older sibling to learn from. Trust was difficult for me. I didn't trust my own feelings, or other people's responses, or that problems could be solved, or that life was for anything but doing school work and chores. As a young adult I knew nothing about how to compromise, stand up for myself, set boundaries, or have my own ideas about what I liked or wanted to do.

I could identify a single feeling I was having but had difficulty figuring out what to do about it; complex feelings were beyond my awareness. I also thought that I caused other people to say, do, and feel things—essentially, that everything was my fault. As a result, I had a lot of negative thoughts about myself. For example, I thought I was stupid, despite being an A+ student. When I tried to avoid the chaos, I was called withdrawn and standoffish. I couldn't figure out where I fit in to the family interactions. They didn't make sense to me.

Skills I Developed

In my quest to be seen and validated by my mother, I was a perfect student, yearbook editor, studied hard, and eventually got a PhD, became a university professor, a therapist, and an author. My mom's typical response was, "We knew you could do it." My dad and grandmother would ask me about my life and work, which felt very validating; however, my mother rarely responded or showed any interest.

I did learn some unique life skills: a highly developed intuition, the ability to be instantly aware of other people's feelings, high degrees of empathy, confidence in my own perspective, and—eventually—an ability to see family behavioral patterns. These were, for me, necessary skills in order to handle my complicated living environment with my three parents—all of whom, it seemed to me, hated as well as loved each other.

I had a passion for trying to understand why people acted the way they did. I wanted to learn how to avoid the landmines in my dealings with my mother. However, she thought trying to understand why things happen was a total waste of time. Knowing more now about how erratically her emotions came and went, I can understand her perspective, but as a teenager, I was shocked that she and I had such different views and values. Her motto was: "I am the way I am, but you better shape up."

Surprisingly, I learned a lot about independence. We lived in the country in the days when children went outside in the morning and only came in for lunch and dinner. Exploring on my own was liberating for me and helped me learn to enjoy the peace and quiet of nature.

When my mother had those dark days of rages or "sick headaches," I couldn't rely on her to solve any problems, understand what I felt, or give me useful advice. She couldn't take care of the house or any of us. So, from first grade on, my sisters and I did dishes, cleaned the house, took care of each other, and learned to find answers on our own—mostly to good effect, but sometimes disastrously.

What I Learned from My Dad

My dad was a highly resilient guy. He was good at solving practical problems and could fix anything around our house. He hung out in the garage a lot, and I always wanted to be out there with him, but my mom would bring us back to the house for chores. He provided the fun in our family with jokes, Sunday afternoon drives, vacations, and his fun-loving brothers and sisters.

I learned endurance from him. I also learned kindness, gentleness, concern, and a desire to be helpful to others. He was rarely ever angry, and I could see his wish that my mother could be somehow healed, but he was at a loss. As a child, I wished he would divorce my mother and take us all away. Years later, after my mother died, I told him that wish, and he simply said that it hadn't been possible. Men just didn't get custody of the children in those days—especially daughters, and he wasn't willing to abandon us. I learned loyalty, persistence, and how to caretake someone with a mental disorder.

What I Learned from My Grandmother

We lived in a small town with one elementary school where my grandmother taught first, second, and third grades. So, she taught me to read, write, do math, and do arts and crafts projects. As I got older, I would get to help her set up her classroom, and years later she eventually came to visit MY classroom. She was busy every moment of every day doing something interesting, and it seemed to me she knew how to do everything. She taught me the practical skills I needed. She was also my first and most powerful model of a strong woman. She was opinionated, determined, educated, as well as compassionate, caring, demonstrably loving, and always reliable. From her, I learned I was loveable and capable.

What Was the Influence of Others?

Although we only saw my father's family once a year, they were my fantasy refuge. As an adult, I moved to California to be closer to them and found a sense of belonging. My mother was an only child, so it had always been just my parents, sisters, and my grandmother growing up.

School was huge for me. I loved learning and found I could succeed well. The effort I put in was rewarded. The logic of math and grammar, as well as the abundance of library stories, carried me into a different world where things made more sense to me. I learned to make friends, deal with differences, be a leader and a follower. I had fun there.

In middle school I took up tap and ballet dance and became a student teacher for the little kids. My dance teacher was a little kooky, independent, happy, enthusiastic, and loved kids. One Christmas she had all the student teachers to her house for a holiday dinner party; it was the first nonfamily dinner I'd ever been to because we rarely did anything with other families. I had a great time. I felt seen and appreciated.

In high school, I really blossomed. It was legitimate for me to be out of the house for school events, be with friends, and go on dates. I felt successful there. The yearbook sponsor became a mentor and someone I could look up to as an independent woman. I wasn't part of the "in crowd," but I felt well liked.

Although I was increasingly free to be on my own, life at home actually got worse. My mother was extremely uneasy and out of sorts as she anticipated my sister and me graduating from high school. She got her first job outside the home, but her rages seemed to increase as things seemed more and more out of her control.

Things fell apart for me just after high school graduation—although I wasn't very aware of it at the time. For years my parents had urged me to go to college, but when the time came, no one knew how to make that happen, and no money had been put aside to pay tuition. So, I went to secretarial school, got pregnant, and married my high school sweetheart.

How It All Worked Out

I played the hero role in my family, but I was also the victim. I took what support I could from around me, but there was a lot to overcome emotionally. I looked good on the outside, but I was scared, and uncertain, confused, and essentially blind to who I was—my strengths, my skills, my shortcomings, and my lack of information about reality. I blundered along. It was also the beginning of the women's movement, and suddenly there were all kinds of new choices, new pressures, and new ways to think about relationships and sex roles to add to my own personal confusion. It was a chaotic time for me.

I finally did go to college, earning my way one year at a time. I got divorced and remarried, and eventually had three daughters of my own. I used to say that I got a PhD and became a therapist because I had spent so many years trying to figure out my crazy family that I just ended up there. I thought I had wandered into this field, but in reality, I've had a passion for decades to truly understand the odd family dynamics of my NP/BP family. Eventually my education taught me how to help others understand these patterns as well. Our families can seem so normal on the outside and are so baffling and confounding to us on the inside. As children we can end up believing there is something wrong with us, unless we have guidance and information to the contrary.

Yes, I spent years in therapy. My biggest aha moment was when my therapist said, "You know, your mom is crazy. It's not you, don't you know?" No, I didn't know until then. Being validated, being seen for who I am, being listened to with interest, being understood, being emotionally supported, and being helped to make decisions changed my life. I often tell parent clients that listening, validating, and providing loving kindnesses will save their children years of therapy and thousands of dollars. It's very true. Much of the therapy that children of a narcissistic or borderline parent actually need is *reparenting*—changing negative thoughts, healing hurt feelings, being listened to, cared about, supported, and encouraged.

I vowed to never parent like my mother. In the early years, I didn't do as well as I would have liked. But I took classes, learned enough to teach parenting skills, and supervised preschool teachers. I learned everything I could. I wanted to break the cycle of dysfunction in my family. As a therapist, I learned how to help families make significant changes. And I put those skills to work with my own children.

Being a good enough, loving, aware, involved, and skilled parent to my three daughters has resulted in three beautiful marriages and happy families. It has turned the legacy of my family of origin from one of hurt, anger, conflict, and misunderstanding into a legacy of caring, love, empathy, strength, and happiness. As I look back at my family history and my many missteps along the way, I'm encouraged that there were enough supportive people, helpful information, generosity, caring, and concern for me to be able to reach a healthy conclusion. It does take a village to raise a child. And thank goodness for that, because the deficits of one parent don't have to be the destiny of any child.

Coming Full Circle: Jean

For a significant portion of my career as a marriage and family therapist, I have specialized in working with divorced families—especially those embroiled in high conflict. Many of these clients were struggling with figuring out how to parent after divorce with an NP/BP parent-partner. Therapists don't always get to see how things turn out in the families they work with. We often are simply one part of a family's support system, and unless we continue to work with our clients for years, we never fully know the results of our work together.

A couple of years ago, I was grocery shopping in my neighborhood store when a woman that looked somewhat familiar approached me. "Do you remember me?" she asked. I must have responded with a vague expression, sort of the "deer in the headlights" look. In truth I was frantically trying to remember how I knew her. She continued by stating her name. "You worked with our family about fifteen years ago." That's when I made the connection. "Oh yes, of course I remember you," I answered. As a psychotherapist I am always concerned about protecting client confidentiality, and quite cautious when I run into clients outside of my office. I offered a smile and waited, letting her take the lead in what might come next. She leaned in closer and said, "I really want to thank you for all you did to help us. I know we weren't an easy family." I smiled again and thanked her for her kind words. I wasn't eager to get into a detailed discussion in the middle of a busy grocery store at the end of a long day, though it was clear that she had more she wanted to say. She gestured toward the small coffee bar in the store. "Do you have a few minutes to talk?" I nodded. "Sure," I said and followed her to a table.

I was beginning to remember the details of this family—mom, dad who had been diagnosed with NPD, and two children, a boy around four, and his sister who was a few years older. It had been a difficult divorce filled with tremendous hostility. Mom ended up leaving the home and taking the kids. Because of her husband's cruel, belittling, and erratic behavior, she'd refused to allow him to see the children. I became involved by order of the court. My task was to reunify dad and his two children, who hadn't seen each other in two years.

It had been a slow process in which I worked to create a safe environment where dad and kids could gradually become reacquainted. It was a series of baby steps that utterly frustrated dad. He wanted things to change NOW. After all, he'd waited two long years and felt vindicated by the court order. Mom wasn't happy about any of it, but she understood the consequences for her if she were to stand in the way. Dad's narcissism made it difficult for him to accept my coaching and suggestions. "I know my own kids better than you could ever know them," he'd say to me. On the one hand he was correct about knowing his children. On another hand, he had no clue about who his children were. He didn't listen, had unrealistic expectations of them, and expected blind obedience, even though the children felt distant from him after the uproar of the divorce and the ensuing two-year separation. The children sometimes balked at coming to our sessions, which irritated their dad. I spent close to three years with this family off and on. When we terminated therapy, I felt I'd done all I could do for the time. The children were older and better able to ask for what they needed/wanted when they were with their dad. Limited parenting time had been reinstated and seemed to be going well. Mom remained vigilant, and dad still wanted things his way.

At the coffee bar, as mom filled me in, I was surprised and pleased to learn that things had actually gone quite well since I'd last seen the family all those years ago. There had been ups and downs, but mainly life had seemed to stabilize for this divorced family. The daughter had recently graduated from college and was headed to the West Coast to work as a high school teacher. Mom proudly reported that their daughter had graduated with honors. She was planning her wedding and had asked dad to walk her down the aisle. And their son was now nineteen years old and living with his dad, still trying to figure out what he wanted to do with his life.

"So, it sounds like you've worked things out," I commented. She laughed and gave an eye roll. "Well, he hasn't changed, just as you predicted. But *we* changed. I knew it was important for the kids to know their dad and spend time with him. You helped us learn how to be more flexible and compassionate, to communicate in ways that didn't create problems, and take care of ourselves."

"I'm glad," I said. "It's inspiring to know that you've fared so well."

She took a sip of her coffee and smiled. "Actually, we *have* fared well. We even held a joint graduation party for our daughter. He and I had dinner several times to plan everything. During those short meetings, I could enjoy the good things about him, and then go home to my sanctuary."

I share this story to demonstrate that time can be a great healer. But it's more than time. I call it "time and." The "and" comes with the work everyone in the family did to make things better. Mom protected her children when they needed her to do that. And she relaxed the boundaries when it was appropriate to do so. They practiced self-compassion and compassion for each other. They learned to be more resilient and accepting. And dad stayed involved, even though at many points along the way he was tempted to quit.

This was a success story and one that can inspire others. There are ways to thrive even in a narcissistic family system. It turned out to be a wonderful gift to me too, since I rarely get to see the end result with families I work with.

Appendix A

Vocabulary of Feeling Words

Table A.1. Vocabulary of Feeling Words

EXCITED	HAPPY	LOVING	CAPABLE
Elated	Glad	Tender	Able
Ecstatic	Contented	Caring	Competent
Thrilled	Grateful	Kind	Skillful
Eager	Pleased	Warm	Ready
Enthusiastic	Delighted	Interested	Prepared
ANGRY	**HOPEFUL**	**COMFORTED**	**RELIEVED**
Disappointed	Wishful	Soothed	Freed
Hurt	Energized	Confident	Liberated
Mad	Encouraged	Supported	Lightened
Scared	Expectant	Thankful	Softened
Rejected	Optimistic	Accepted	Calmed
UPSET	**SURPRISED**	**CONFUSED**	**USED**
Worried	Amazed	Uncertain	Manipulated
Anxious	Bewildered	Insecure	Tricked
Fearful	Shocked	Puzzled	Betrayed
Troubled	Devastated	Shaken up	Cheated
Awkward	Unprepared	Floundering	Gullible
SAD	**DEFENSIVE**	**ATTACKED**	**RESILIENT**
Distressed	Guarded	Blamed	Strong
Hurt	Avoiding	Accused	Competent
Pained	Fearful	Condemned	Self-assured
Forlorn	Evading	Reprimanded	Adaptable
Low	Desperate	Rejected	Durable

~

Appendix B

Communication Prompts

Opening

- What's on your mind?
- What have you been thinking about?

Problem

- What's worrying you?
- Are you having a problem?
- What's troubling you?

More Information

- Tell me about it.
- Can you fill me in?
- What have you tried so far?

Feelings

- How do you feel about that?
- What do you make of that?

Example

- Can you give me an example?
- In what way?
- Like what?

More

- Can you tell me more?
- Anything else?
- What else are you feeling?

Exploring

- How does this affect you?
- What did you say/do?
- How do you fit into this?

Clarification

- What seems confusing to you?
- What doesn't seem to make sense?

Hypothesizing

- What do you suppose is happening?
- Why would a person act that way?
- If you had your choice, what would you do?

~

Appendix C

Suggested Reading

Positive Parenting

Dreikurs, Rudolf, and Vicki Soltz. *Children the Challenge*. New York: Penguin Group, 2004.

Faber, Adele, and Elaine Mazlish. *How to Talk so Kids Will Listen and Listen so Kids Will Talk*. New York: Scribner, 2012.

Glenn, H. Stephen, and Jane Nelson. *Raising Self-Reliant Children in a Self-Indulgent World*. New York: Three Rivers Press, 2000.

Goleman, Daniel. *Emotional Intelligence* (10th ed.). New York: Random House Publishing Group, 2006.

Gordon, Thomas. *Parent Effectiveness Training*. New York: Three Rivers Press, 2000.

Gottman, John, and Daniel Goleman. *Raising an Emotionally Intelligent Child*. New York: Simon & Schuster, 2011.

Louis, John Philip, and Karen M. Louis. *Good Enough Parenting*. New York: Morgan James Publisher, 2015.

Lythcott-Haims, Julie. *How to Raise an Adult: Break Free of the Overparenting Trap and Prepare Your Kid for Success*. New York: St. Martin's Griffin, 2015.

Steinberg, Laurence. *10 Basic Principles of Good Parenting*. New York: Simon & Schuster, 2004.

Tsabary, Shefali. *The Conscious Parent: Transforming Ourselves, Empowering Our Children*. Vancouver, Canada: Namaste Publishing, 2010.

Young, Karen. "Building Resilience in Children—20 Practical, Powerful Strategies (Backed by Science)." http://heysigmund.com.

Resilience

Altman, Donald. *101 Mindful Ways to Build Resilience, Cultivate Calm, Clarity, Optimism & Happiness Each Day*. Eau Claire, WI: PESI Publishing and Media, 2016.

Graham, Linda. *Bouncing Back: Rewiring Your Brain for Maximum Resilience and Well-Being*. Novato, CA: New World Library, 2013.

———. *Resilience: Powerful Practices for Bouncing Back from Disappointment, Difficulty and Even Disaster*. Novato, CA: New World Library, 2018.

Hanson, Rick. *Hardwiring Happiness: The New Brain Science of Contentment, Calm, and Confidence*. New York: Harmony Books, 2016.

Hanson, Rick, and Forest Hanson. *Resilient: How to Grow an Unsinkable Core of Calm, Strength, and Happiness*. New York: Harmony Books, 2018.

Lee, Cindi. "The Joy of Self-Caring." *Lions Roar*, May 2019.

Neff, Kristin. *Self-Compassion: Stop Beating Yourself Up and Leave Insecurity Behind*. New York: Harper Collins, 2011.

Neff, Kristin, and Christopher Germer. *The Mindful Self-Compassion Workbook: A Proven Way to Accept Yourself, Build Inner Strength and Thrive*. New York: The Guilford Press, 2018.

Young, Karen. "Building Resilience in Children—20 Practical, Powerful Strategies (Backed by Science)." http://heysigmund.com.

For Adults with Narcissistic/Borderline Parents

Brown, Nina. *Children of the Self-Absorbed: A Grown-Up's Guide to Getting Over Narcissistic Parents*. Oakland, CA: New Harbinger, 2008.

Gibson. Lindsey. *Adult Children of Emotionally Immature Parents: How to Heal from Distant, Rejecting, Self-Absorbed Parents*. Oakland, CA: New Harbinger, 2015.

Golomb, Elan. *Trapped in the Mirror: Adult Children of Narcissistic Parents in Their Struggle for Self*. New York: William Morrow & Co. 1995.

Lawson, Christine. *Understanding the Borderline Mother: Helping Her Children Transcend the Intense, Unpredictable and Volatile Relationship*. Lanham, MD: Rowman & Littlefield, 2004.

McBride, Karyl. *Will I Ever Be Good Enough?: Healing Daughters of Narcissistic Mothers*. New York: Free Press., 2009

Roth, Kimberlee, and Freda Friedman. *Surviving a Borderline Parent: How to Heal Your Childhood Wounds & Build Trust, Boundaries, and Self-Esteem*. Oakland, CA: New Harbinger, 2013.

Notes

Chapter One

1. Gregory Lester, *Advanced Diagnosis, Treatment and Management of DSM-5 Personality Disorders* (Houston: Ashcroft Press; Wisconsin: PESI, 2018).

2. Karolinska Institute, https://ki.se/en/research/the-swedish-twin-registry.

3. Stephanie Donaldson-Pressman and Robert M. Pressman, *The Narcissistic Family: Diagnosis and Treatment* (San Francisco: Josey-Bass Publishers, 2009).

4. Simon Baron-Cohen, *Zero Degrees of Empathy* (New York: Penguin Group, 2011).

5. Donaldson-Pressman and Pressman, *The Narcissistic Family*.

6. Nina Brown, *Children of the Self Absorbed: A Grown-Up's Guide to Getting Over Narcissistic Parents* (Oakland, CA: New Harbinger, 2008).

Chapter Two

1. Paul Mason and Randi Kreger, *Stop Walking on Eggshells* (2nd ed.) (Oakland, CA: New Harbinger, 2010).

2. Christine Lawson, *Understanding the Borderline Mother* (Lanham, MD: Rowman & Littlefield, 2004).

3. Lawson, *Understanding the Borderline Mother*.

4. Annie Wright, "How to Recover from Growing Up with a Narcissistic Parent," https://anniewrightpsychotherapy.com, May 27, 2018.

5. Rudolf Dreikurs and Vicki Soltz, *Children the Challenge* (New York: Penguin Group, 2004).

Chapter Three

1. Margalis Fjelstad, *Stop Caretaking the Borderline or Narcissist: How to Get Out of the Drama and Get on with Life* (Lanham: MD: Rowman & Littlefield, 2013).

Chapter Four

1. Julie Hall, *The Narcissist in Your Life: Recognizing the Patterns and Learning to Break Free* (New York: Hatchett Book Group, Inc., 2019).
2. Paul Mason and Randi Kreger, *Stop Walking on Eggshells* (Oakland, CA: New Harbinger Press, 2010).
3. Weinberger Divorce & Family Law Group, https//wwwweinbergerlawgroup.com/blog.

Chapter Five

1. Bonnie Badenoch, *Being a Brain-Wise Therapist: A Practical Guide to Interpersonal Neurobiology* (New York: W. W. Norton, 2008).
2. Substance Abuse and Mental Health Services Administration, https://www.samhsa.gov.
3. Linda Graham, *Resilience: Powerful Practices for Bouncing Back from Disappointment, Difficulty, and Even Disaster* (Novato, CA: New World Library, 2018).

Chapter Six

1. Kristin Neff and Christopher Germer, *The Mindful Self-Compassion Workbook: A Proven Way to Accept Yourself, Build Inner Strength and Thrive* (New York: The Guilford Press, 2018); Margalis Fjelstad, *Healing from a Narcissistic Relationship: A Caretaker's Guide to Recovery, Empowerment & Transformation* (Lanham, MD: Rowman & Littlefield, 2017).

Chapter Seven

1. www.verywellfamily.com/feelings-words.

Chapter Eight

1. Kristen Neff, *Self-Compassion: Stop Beating Yourself Up and Leave Insecurity Behind* (New York: Harper Collins, 2011).

2. Neff, *Self-Compassion*.

3. H. Stephen Glenn and Jane Nelson, *Raising Self-Reliant Children in a Self-Indulgent World* (New York: Three Rivers Press, 2000).

Chapter Nine

1. Brin Grenyer, "Project Air: Family, Partner and Carer Intervention Manual for Personality Disorders," www.projectairstrategy.org.

2. Mary Ainsworth, M. C. Blehar, E. Waters, and S. Wall, *Patterns of Attachment* (Hillsdale, NY: Psychology Press, 1978).

3. Kristen Neff, "How Self-Compassion Changes Everything," interview on Sounds True with Tammy Simon, www.soundstrue.com.

4. Linda Graham, *Resilience: Powerful Practices for Bouncing Back from Disappointment, Difficulty and Even Disaster* (Novato, CA: New World Library, 2018).

Chapter Ten

1. Sue Johnson, *Love Sense: The Revolutionary New Science of Romantic Relationships* (New York: Little Brown, 2013).

2. Rick Hanson and Forest Hanson, *Resilient: How to Grown an Unshakable Core of Calm, Strength, and Happiness* (New York: Harmony Books, 2016).

Chapter Eleven

1. Kristen Neff, *Self-Compassion: The Proven Power of Being Kind to Yourself* (New York: Harper Collins, 2015).

2. Tim Desmond, *Self-Compassion in Psychotherapy: Mindfulness Based Practices for Healing and Transformation* (New York: W. W. Norton, 2016).

3. Tim Desmond, *The Self-Compassion Skills Workbook: A 14-Day Plan to Transform Your Relationship with Yourself* (New York: W. W. Norton, 2017).

4. Linda Graham, *Resilience: Powerful Practices for Bouncing Back from Disappointment, Difficulty, and Even Disaster* (Novato, CA: New World Library, 2018).

5. Gail Silver, "How to Practice Metta with Children," https://lionsroar.com. 8/1/2018.

6. Emma Seppala, "A Gift of Loving Kindness Meditation," https://emmaseppala.com/gift-loving-kindness-meditation. 5/28/2014.

Chapter Twelve

1. John Gottman, *Raising an Emotionally Intelligent Child* (New York: Simon & Schuster, 1997).

2. Diane Poole Heller, *The Power of Attachment: How to Create Deep and Lasting Intimate Relationships* (Boulder, CO: Sounds True, 2019).

Chapter Thirteen

1. Kristin Neff, *Self-Compassion: Stop Beating Yourself Up and Leave Insecurity Behind* (New York: Harper Collins, 2011).

Chapter Sixteen

1. Karyl McBride, *Will I Ever Be Free of You?: How to Negotiate a High-Conflict Divorce from a Narcissist and Heal Your Family* (New York: Atria Books, 2015).

2. John Gottman and Robert Levenson, https://www.gottman.com/about/research/.

Chapter Nineteen

1. W. Thomas Boyce, *The Orchid and the Dandelion: Why Some Children Struggle and How All Can Thrive* (New York: Alfred A. Knopf, 2019).

2. Julie Lythcott-Haims, *How to Raise an Adult: Break Free of the Overparenting Trap and Prepare Your Kid for Success* (New York: St. Martin's Press, 2015).

3. Gregg Henriques, "Keep Calm ad Carry On," *Psychology Today*, May/June, 2018.

4. Linda Graham, *Bouncing Back: Rewiring Your Brain for Maximum Resilience and Well-Being* (Novato, CA: New World Library, 2013).

5. Diana Baumrind, "Authoritative Parenting: Characteristics and Effects," https://verywellmind.com/what-is-authortative-parenting-2794956.

6. Linda Graham, *Resilience: Powerful Practices for Bouncing Back from Disappointment, Difficulty, and Even Disaster* (Novato, CA: New World Library, 2013).

7. W. Clement Stone, *The Success System That Never Fails* (New York: BN Publishing, 2012).

Bibliography

Ainsworth, M., M. C. Blehar, E. Waters, and S. Wall. *Patterns of Attachment: A Psychological Study of the Strange Situation.* New Jersey: Erlbaum.

Altman, Donald. *101 Mindful Ways to Build Resilience, Cultivate Calm, Clarity, Optimism & Happiness Each Day.* Eau Claire, WI: PESI Publishing and Media, 2016.

Badenoch, Bonnie. *Being a Brain Wise Therapist: A Practical Guide to Interpersonal Neurobiology.* New York: W. W. Norton, 2008.

Baker, Amy J. L., and Paul R. Fine. *Co-Parenting with a Toxic Ex: What to Do When Your Ex-Spouse Tries to Turn the Kids Against You.* Oakland, CA: New Harbinger, 2014.

Baron-Cohen, Simon. *Zero Degrees of Empathy.* New York: Penguin Group, 2011.

Behrman, Lauren J., and Jeffrey Zimmerman. *Loving Your Children More Than You Hate Each Other: Powerful Tools for Navigating a High-Conflict Divorce.* Oakland, CA: New Harbinger, 2018.

Boyce, W. Thomas. "Orchids and Dandelions." *Psychology Today*, January/February, 2019.

———. *Why Some Children Struggle and How All Can Thrive.* New York: Alfred A. Knopf, 2019.

Brown, Nina. *Children of the Self-Absorbed: A Grown-Up's Guide to Getting Over Narcissistic Parents.* Oakland, CA: New Harbinger, 2008.

Cherry, Kendra. "Characteristics of Resilient People." https://www.verywellmind.com.

Desmond, Tim. *Self-Compassion in Psychotherapy: Mindfulness-Based Practices for Healing and Transformation.* New York: W. W. Norton, 2015.

———. *The Self-Compassion Skills Workbook: A 14-Day Plan to Transform Your Relationship with Yourself.* New York: W. W. Norton, 2017.

Donaldson-Pressman, Stephanie, and Robert M. Pressman. *The Narcissistic Family: Diagnosis and Treatment.* San Francisco: Josey-Bass Publishers, 2009.

Dreikurs, Rudolf, and Vicki Soltz. *Children the Challenge.* New York: Penguin Group, 2004.

Eddy, Bill, and Randi Kreger. *Splitting: Protecting Yourself While Divorcing Someone with Borderline or Narcissistic Personality Disorder.* Oakland, CA: New Harbinger, 2011.

Evans, Patricia. *The Verbally Abusive Relationship: How to Recognize and It and How to Respond* (2nd ed.). Massachusetts: Adams Media Corp., 1996.

Faber, Adele, and Elaine Mazlish. *How to Talk so Kids Will Listen and Listen so Kids Will Talk.* New York: Scribner, 2012.

Farzad, B. Robert. "How to Protect Your Child from a Narcissistic Father or Mother." http://farzadlaw.com.

Fjelstad, Margalis. *Healing from a Narcissistic Relationship: A Caretaker's Guide to Recovery, Empowerment & Transformation.* Lanham, MD: Rowman & Littlefield, 2017.

———. *Stop Caretaking the Borderline or Narcissist: How to Get Out of the Drama and Get on with Life.* Lanham, MD: Rowman & Littlefield, 2013.

———. *The Borderline, the Narcissist & YOU: Learning to Let Go of Caretaking.* On-line course. Cartaker.digitalchalk.com.

Germer, Christopher K., and K. D. Neff. "Self-Compassion in Clinical Practice." *Journal of Clinical Psychology* 69, no. 8 (2013).

——— and Sharon Salzburg. *The Mindful Path to Self-Compassion.* New York: The Guilford Press, 2009.

Gibson. Lindsey. *Adult Children of Emotionally Immature Parents: How to Heal from Distant, Rejecting, Self-Absorbed Parents.* Oakland, CA: New Harbinger, 2015.

Glenn, H. Stephen, and Jane Nelson. *Raising Self-Reliant Children in a Self-Indulgent World.* New York: Three Rivers Press, 2000.

Goleman, Daniel. *Emotional Intelligence* (10th ed.). New York: Random House Publishing Group, 2006.

Golomb, Elan. *Trapped in the Mirror: Adult Children of Narcissistic Parents in Their Struggle for Self.* New York: William Morrow & Co. 1995.

Gordon, Thomas. *Parent Effectiveness Training.* New York: Three Rivers Press, 2000.

Gottman, John, and Joan Declaire. *Raising an Emotionally Intelligent Child*. New York: Simon & Schuster, 1997.

―――― and Robert Levinson. "Marriage and Couples." The Gottman Institute. https://www.gottman.com/about/research/couples/.

―――― and Nan Silver. *The Seven Principles for Making Marriage Work*. New York: Random House, 2015.

Graham, Linda. *Bouncing Back: Rewiring Your Brain for Maximum Resilience and Well-Being*. Novato, CA: New World Library, 2013.

――――. *Resilience: Powerful Practices for Bouncing Back from Disappointment, Difficulty and Even Disaster*. Novato, CA: New World Library, 2018.

Gunderson, John G., and Cynthia Berkowitz. "Supporting a Loved-One with Borderline Personality Disorder." Facing the Facts. www.bpdfamily.com.

Hall, Julie L. "How to Protect Your Children from Your Narcissist Spouse." https://huffingtonpost.com.

――――. *The Narcissist in Your Life: Recognizing the Patterns and Learning to Break Free*. New York: Hachette Book Group, 2019.

Hanson, Rick. *Hardwiring Happiness: The New Brain Science of Contentment, Calm, and Confidence*. New York: Harmony Books, 2016.

―――― and Forest Hanson. *Resilient: How to Grow an Unsinkable Core of Calm, Strength, and Happiness*. New York: Harmony Books, 2018.

Harvey, Pat, and Jeanine Penzo. *Parenting a Child Who Has Intense Emotions*. Oakland, CA: New Harbinger, 2009.

HealthyPlace.com Staff Writer. "Issues for Parents with Mental Illness." https://www.healthyplace.com/parenting/parents-with-mental-illness.

Henriques, Gregg. "Keep Calm and Carry On." Psychology Today, May/June 2018.

Howes, C., and S. Ritchie. "Attachment Organization in Children with Difficult Life Circumstances." *Developmental Psychopathology* 11: 251–68.

Johnson, Sue. *Love Sense: The Revolutionary New Science of Romantic Relationships*. New York: Little. Brown and Company, 2013.

Kennedy, Janice H., and Charles E. Kennedy. "Attachment Theory: Implications for School Psychology." *Psychology in the Schools* 41, no. 2 (2004).

Knight Raskin, Molly. "When Passion Is the Enemy." *Scientific American Mind*, July/August, 2010.

Lamont, Andrea. "Mothers with Borderline Personality Disorder." *Graduate Student Journal of Psychology* 8 (2006).

Lawson, Christine. *Understanding the Borderline Mother: Helping Her Children Transcend the Intense, Unpredictable and Volatile Relationship*. Lanham, MD: Rowman & Littlefield, 2004.

Lee, Cindi. "The Joy of Self-Caring." *Lion's Roar*, May 2019.

Lester, Gregory W. *Advanced Diagnosis, Treatment and Management of DSM-5 Personality Disorders*. Houston: Ashcroft Press and Wisconsin: PESI, 2018.

———. *Power with People: How to Handle Just About Anyone to Accomplish Just About Anything*. Houston: Ashcroft Press, 2015.

Lewis, Chris. "Co-Parenting with a Former Spouse with Mental Illness." http://www.mariadroste.org/resources/articles.

Lewis, John P., and Karen M. Louis. *Good Enough Parenting*. New York: Morgan James Publishers, 2015.

Lythcott-Haims, Julie. *How to Raise an Adult: Break Free of the Overparenting Trap and Prepare Your Kid for Success*. New York: St. Martin's Griffin, 2015.

Mason, Paul, and Randi Kreger. *Stop Walking on Eggshells* (2nd ed.). Oakland, CA: New Harbinger, 2010.

Matthes, Rebecca. "We the Couple: Gestures Important for Fostering Satisfaction." *Psychology Today*, November/December 2018.

McBride, Jean. *Talking to Children About Divorce*. Althea Press, 2016.

McBride, Karyl. "The Real Effect of Narcissistic Parenting on Children." https://narcissistabusesupport.com.

———. *Will I Ever Be Free of You?: How to Navigate a High-Conflict Divorce from a Narcissist and Heal Your Family*. New York: Atria Books, 2015.

———. *Will I Ever Be Good Enough?: Healing Daughters of Narcissistic Mothers*. New York: Free Press, 2009. .

Mead, Sarah. "7 Key Characteristics of Resilient Children." https://wwwwhitbyschool.org.

Meyers, Seth. "Narcissistic Parents' Psychological Effect on Their Children." www.psychologytoday.com/blog.

Neff, Kristin. *Self-Compassion: Stop Beating Yourself Up and Leave Insecurity Behind*. New York: Harper Collins, 2011.

Neff, Kristin, and Christopher Germer. *The Mindful Self-Compassion Workbook: A Proven Way to Accept Yourself, Build Inner Strength and Thrive*. New York: The Guilford Press, 2018.

Nicola, Joanna. *The Nicola Method Workbook for Partners of High-Conflict Women*. www.nicolamethodforhighconflict.com.

Oaklander, Mandy. "How to Bounce Back." *The Science of Happiness: New Discoveries for a More Joyful Life*. TIME, Inc. Specials 2018.

Pedro-Carroll, JoAnne. *Putting Children First: Proven Strategies for Helping Children Thrive Through Divorce*. New York: Avery, 2010.

Pillay, Srini. "Greater Self-Acceptance Improves Emotional Well-Being." https://www.health.harvard.edu.

Pincott, Jena. "Your Inner Critic and Self Compassion." *Psychology Today*, May/June 2019.

Poole Heller, Diane. *The Power of Attachment: How to Create Deep and Lasting Intimate Relationships.* Boulder, CO: Sounds True, 2018.

Project Air: *Strategy for Personality Disorders: Family, Partner and Carer Intervention Manual for Personality Disorders.* Wollongong: University of Wollongong, Illawarra Health and Medical Research Institute. AU, 2016. www.projectairstrategy.org.

Rodman, Samantha. *How to Talk to Your Kids About Your Divorce: Effective Communication Techniques for Your Changing Family.* Adams Media, 2015.

Ross, Julie, and Judy Corcoran. *Joint Custody with a Jerk: Raising a Child with an Un-Cooperative Ex.* New York: St. Martin's Press, 2011.

Roth, Kimberlee, and Freda Friedman. *Surviving a Borderline Parent: How to Heal Your Childhood Wounds & Build Trust, Boundaries, and Self Esteem.* Oakland, CA: New Harbinger, 2013.

Schwartz, Allan. "The Narcissistic Parent." https://www.mentalhelp.net.

Seppala, Emma. "A Gift of Loving Kindness Meditation." https://emmaseppala.com.

Siegel, Daniel, and Tina Payne Bryson. *The Whole-Brain Child: 12 Revolutionary Strategies to Nurture Your Child's Developing Mind.* New York: Bantam Books, 2012.

Silver, Gail. "How to Practice Metta with Children." https://lionsroarcom.

Steinberg, Laurence. *10 Basic Principles of Good Parenting.* New York: Simon & Schuster, 2004.

Stepp, Stephanie, Diana Whalen, Paul Pilkonis, Alison Hipwell, and Michele Levine. "Children of Mothers with Borderline Personality Disorder: Identifying Parenting Behaviors as Potential Targets for Intervention." *Personal Discord* 3, no. 1 (2011: 76–91.

Tsabary, Shefali. *The Conscious Parent: Transforming Ourselves, Empowering Our Children.* Vancouver, CA: Namaste Publishing, 2010.

Weinberger Divorce & Family Law Group. "Preparing for Your Day in Court." www.weibergerlawgroup.com/blog.

Wright, Annie. "How to Recover from Growing Up with a Narcissistic Parent." https://anniewrightpsychotherapy.com. May 27, 2018.

Young, Karen. "Building Resilience in Children—20 Practical, Powerful Strategies (Backed by Science)." http://heysigmund.com.

Index

~

About the Authors

Margalis Fjelstad, PhD, LMFT, has been a therapist for over thirty-five years specializing in the care of people who have been negatively affected by a narcissistic or borderline family member. She is the author of *Stop Caretaking the Borderline or Narcissist: How to End the Drama and Get on with Life* and *Healing from a Narcissistic Relationship: A Caretaker's Guide to Recovery, Empowerment, and Transformation.* Her goal is to help families impacted by these personality disorders to function more effectively and become healthier and happier. You can find more information and subscribe to her Caretaker Recovery Newsletter at www.margalistherapy.com. Dr. Fjelstad can be reached at margalistherapy@gmail.com. She is also available for phone consultations.

Jean McBride, MS, LMFT, is a licensed marriage and family therapist in private practice in Fort Collins, Colorado. She has worked with individuals and families dealing with divorce, parenting after divorce, and remarriage for thirty years. She has developed curriculum and taught court-ordered parenting classes to over twenty thousand divorcing parents. She is the author of *Encouraging Words for New Stepmothers* and *Talking to Children about Divorce.* She can be reached at her website: divorcehelpforparents.com. She is also available for phone consultations.